God SHED HIS Grace ON THEE

The Christian Foundations of America and
Your Responsibility as a Christian to Continue the Pursuit

REXFORD "REX" LOUTH

WestBow
PRESS
A DIVISION OF THOMAS NELSON

Unless otherwise noted, all scripture quoted herein is taken from the New King James Version®. Copyright © 1982 by Thomas Nelson, Inc. Used by permission. All rights reserved.

WestBow Press books may be ordered through booksellers or by contacting:

WestBow Press
A Division of Thomas Nelson
1663 Liberty Drive
Bloomington, IN 47403
www.westbowpress.com
1 (866) 928-1240

Because of the dynamic nature of the Internet, any web addresses or links contained in this book may have changed since publication and may no longer be valid. The views expressed in this work are solely those of the author and do not necessarily reflect the views of the publisher, and the publisher hereby disclaims any responsibility for them.

Any people depicted in stock imagery provided by Thinkstock are models, and such images are being used for illustrative purposes only. Certain stock imagery © Thinkstock.

ISBN: 978-1-4908-1453-7 (sc)
ISBN: 978-1-4908-1454-4 (hc)
ISBN: 978-1-4908-1455-1 (e)

Library of Congress Control Number: 2013919953

Printed in the United States of America.

WestBow Press rev. date: 3/12/2014

Contents

Dedication

This book is dedicated to my wife, Janet,
who has stood by my side
since September 29, 1979. She has been my friend,
my constant support, and the love of my life.
She heard every update on my progress
throughout the writing of this manuscript,
and was watching as I typed the final sentences.

And to my parents, Rev. Donald and Sharon Louth,
who have believed in me my entire life,
gave me my foundation in Christ,
and caused me to believe I could accomplish
whatever God had for me.
I love you!

Acknowledgements

I wish to thank all of those who contributed time, resources and effort into assisting with the publication of this book. The finalized cover art is presented by my son-in-law Chris. He took my idea and ran with it, providing the perfect scene for what I was attempting to convey. The final edit and assistance with formatting came from a great friend, Rebecca Blair. The "Author's Photo" was taken and professionally finished by Larry and Ruth Mead with Mead Photography, whom I have come to appreciate and become good and fast friends with. May our friendship just continue to grow from this moment and forward.

There are so many who have inspired me over the years that I dare not begin to mention those by name, but there are those in ministry who have supported me in helping develop me into the pastor, preacher, and minister I have become today. In addition, the political leaders who helped bring me into the work of politics, and help support me today as colleagues and friends, including Colorado State Representatives and Senators, and the United States Congressman of the 5th Congressional District here in Colorado. So many have been there working side-by-side in the pursuit of establishing the moral principles upon which the people of any community must rely. And Randy Wilson, my friend who helped involve me in the national effort to raise the standard of Christ in the political world.

My family has been so amazing since taking on this project. They have been so excited for me; each one asking where I was in the process along every step of the way. My mom, dad, and brothers and sister, and their families, have issued encouragement at every turn. My children and their families have contributed so much to keeping me on pace and "in the zone". My daughter Stephanie even read the completed work before anyone else and helped edit the final version.

Of course, my wife is the ever supportive friend whom I have loved since high school. She has given me strength to believe in what I could do when I doubted. She put up with my "and then I brought out…" and my "I just want to complete this part before I finish tonight." She stood at my side with her hand on my shoulder as I typed the final sentence of the manuscript. I could not have done this without her.

And, finally, I give all the glory to God. He knew what I was to be even before I was conceived. It is His love that sent Jesus Christ to this earth to die for my sin. It is at His urging that I even took this on. And without Him, I could do nothing. But with Him… well… "I can do all things through Christ who strengthens me." (Philippians 4:13)

Foreword

A few years ago I attended a gathering of concerned citizens regarding the direction of our country. There was a great lineup of speakers - a retired Delta Force Commander, a retired Marine Colonel, a US Senator and a long time pastor and well known author - that brought a unique cultural perspective. Each speaker concluded that the true leaders of this country - We The People - must rise and take our place of leadership starting at the local level; in our communities where God has placed us.

This is where I met Rex Louth, a pastor and one of the concerned folks on the floor of the arena where this event was held. As we talked, I found Rex was already doing the work of calling others in the community to know our history as a nation, understand how blessed we are as a people and to do their duty by being informed on the issues of the day, holding our elected officials accountable and working to find likeminded people who had a call on their lives to run for office.

As I got to know Rex I saw he was a man of history particularly of our founding days as a nation and of the Civil War.

I also found Rex was a pastor who is not afraid to speak the truth from the pulpit and relate what the Bible says about the cultural issues of the day. As I have traveled the country over the last couple of decades, I hear the people crying out for their pastors to "connect the dots" for them. They want to know the how the Bible speaks to everyday situations so they can enter into the conversations around the water cooler or with other parents at the sporting events their children are participating in. People today intuitively know America is off track, but have not realized the agenda in public education is to lessen the teaching of our true American history, or worse yet to rewrite the truth of our country's founding. As a people we are working hard to make ends meet, raise our children and live respectful lives only to realize we don't even know who we are as a nation. Now Hosea 4:6 jumps in our face when we read, "My people are destroyed for a lack of knowledge." When our children ask what America stands for or who America is as a nation, we realize we don't know who we are, we don't know where we have come from and consequently, as the old saying goes, we don't know where to go from here. This is the question so many are asking today; what does the future hold? Will we give our children something better than we were given by our parents? The truth today is, the majority doesn't know what they believe or should believe about who and what America is.

As I travel the country interacting with pastors and community leaders I see we as a people have lost the basics of why people from around the world have come and today are still coming to America... to live in freedom. The Pilgrims came to worship their God as they felt compelled and to live responsible orderly lives. Others came as entrepreneurs looking for opportunities to create and do business without the over burdensome taxation of a Monarchy. Some came to escape the Cass system, own their own property and live in freedom to create what has come to be known as the "American Dream." However, today the American Dream has been hijacked by materialism that has defined success as having the nicest, biggest and most of all the world has to offer.

This book, *God Shed His Grace On Thee*, calls us back to what has attracted people to America from around the world; the torch bearer of freedom, the liberators of oppression and a nation that is Christian at its roots. Rex reminds us that God put Israel at the crossroads of culture so they might influence the world and point them to the God who is their Creator. God calls us to do the same, but we must know the truth, we must be diligent in studying the truth for "the truth will set us free." It will set us free from the discouragement of culture, the despair because of our economy and the uncertainty of our times. Knowing the truth we can help set others free from the cares of this world. Knowing the Kingdom work we can live out the Genesis mandate to be fruitful and multiply as we rule and subdue this fallen world. Will God give this country back to us as we have known it? I don't know, but we can ask. We can start conversations with others and encourage them to do the same. We can remind each other of God's Word that says to "pray for the city in which I have lead you into captivity. So that if it prospers, you too may prosper." Jeremiah 29:7

I am reminded of what Samuel Adams said, "It does not take a majority to prevail, but rather an irate, tireless minority keen on setting brush fires of freedom in the minds of men." I have been in DC with Rex more than once, in his office and at other gatherings where brush fires of freedom are being set ablaze. I can assure you, Rex is one of the tireless, investing all he has to restore a nation that was birthed to allow the masses a place of freedom to raise the generations to come. This book will inspire you to do the same. Spread the word!

Randy Wilson

National Field Director
Family Research Council
Washington, DC

Introduction

America, America, God shed His grace on thee... Has He? Is He? Will He continue to do so? Is this land of freedom divinely ordained? Did God fashion this nation with intention in the forge of both natural and man-made struggles? These are the questions that burn in the souls of men and women across this nation. These are at the center of a raging debate which has answers imbedded in the actions of those who passed through treacherous seas and encountered native peril in a foreign territory. They pursued their quest at immense personal risk, setting their very lives as equity in order to find the hope of freedom. And what freedom drove them forward? The freedom to serve God in a manner of their choosing.

The explorers of the 15th and 16th centuries defied the commonly accepted theories of their time and set sail in pursuit of their dreams to reach across the globe to trade with what is known today as the Far East. And, as was the case in later colonization efforts, each brought along their faith. In their discoveries, they made a mark on the new land by establishing a presence reflecting their particular approach to worship. Once it was known that new continents awaited them, established nations raced to plant footholds there. And while those priorities which drove kingdoms and nations to lay claim to the new found territory were based in financial gain, each endeavor was accompanied by a Christian contingent.

In addition to nations moving toward colonization, oppressive theocracies in Europe pressured their citizens to conduct themselves in worship according to their expectations or be imprisoned, beaten, and even martyred. As a result, leaders of Christian congregations from all over began to formulate plans to travel to the "New World". Fully aware of the hardships that awaited them on the journey and in braving the untamed wilderness, these souls determined to serve God freely as they wished and face whatever may come their way. Many did not survive the harsh conditions aboard the cramped quarters of the tall ships. Families were torn apart or completely lost in the attempt to find freedom.

In all these things, they were more than conquerors. Each wave of inhabitants coming upon America's shores expanded the spiritual influence in unique ways. Within the next few decades the Puritans, Quakers, and other groups wishing freedom in religious practice braved the arduous trek across more than 3,500 miles of contrary ocean currents to set foot on shores offering freedom to worship their Heavenly Father as they chose. They established the foundation for you and me to be able to serve the Lord in our own way, unfettered by a government-sanctioned religion.

Since those early days of the American Experience, the commission to "Go into all the world" has continued across the continent and back around the planet. In each phase of taming the environment from coast to coast, brave men and women committed to their faith ensured the message of Christ would go wherever the citizens settled. And missionaries from the United States have traveled to even the most remote points, bringing Christianity to everyone.

Now a new era has arisen. A surge of humanism, atheistic at its very core, threatens the moral compass by which we lived for the first two centuries. The Bible calls such times "perilous." A new *morality* has supplanted the long held codes of decency. And Christians are now told to be quiet in the public square.

"History is written by the victors," is a phrase commonly attributed to Winston Churchill, but is, in truth, of unknown origin. I offer the statement that "History is rewritten by those angered by the truth." Much has been written of recent decades regarding the "truth" of the founding of the United States of America. Those not wishing to acknowledge the Christian undergirding of this nation have chosen to cite statements of those living during the years of America's formation, that they have either taken out of context, or do not represent the general ideals of the Founding Fathers.

It is time to rise above the noise created to disquiet the believer. It is time to "Cry aloud, spare not; Lift up your voice like a trumpet; Tell (His) people their transgression..." (Isaiah 58:1) The Christian message is the one true gospel. God is calling for a new commitment: to change what we can, praying for guidance and strength to do and teach what is right, like those courageous travelers of centuries past.

MAYFLOWER II
Replica of the Mayflower
Plimoth Plantation – Plymouth, Massachusetts

For God and Country

Standing forward atop the forecastle of the ship, he scans the seemingly endless silver and blue horizon before him just beyond the bowsprit of the wooden vessel carrying him onward. Attempting to appear unhindered by the many days and leagues which have passed since the expedition left the familiar shores of home, he stands firmly in place. His acute perception of the men's restlessness causes a twinge of concern, but he is convinced he can persuade them to press onward.

His mind wanders briefly to the stories of sea monsters and world's end. Many such excursions have never returned. It was anyone's guess what fate took the previous crews. All he knows is that he is certain that the objective of his quest lies just beyond that horizon.

This is the life of the explorer. And by the mid-1400's many scholars were convinced the world was round. Prior expeditions into the unknown Westward pursuit of the orient had failed, and no one knew why. The richest commodities of the day were brought back from merchant voyages to China, India, and other lands of Southeast Asia. But there was no easy or quick route. In addition to these facts, wars also raged between the great nations of the day. Mighty kingdoms fought for supremacy on the seas and land.

To this historical time arose explorers, convinced that the fastest and most profitable way to get to the east was by means of traveling westward. Scientists of the day agreed that the earth was, indeed, round. Men who had sailed aboard the various merchant tours on the arduous journeys southward and ultimately around Africa's southernmost tip believed there had to be a better way.

One such man was Cristoforo Colombo, better known to the world today as Christopher Columbus. Born in Genoa, present day Italy, sometime between late August and the end of October, 1454, Columbus grew to become a nautical master. He began making the sea his lifestyle when just a teenager. He was part of many trade voyages throughout the Mediterranean and Aegean seas. As he grew older, he began serving on ships taking expeditions to Africa. The knowledge he gained of the ocean and wind currents allowed him to develop the concept of sailing westward toward the Far East.

Columbus was determined to prove his theories of the flow of the waterways between modern day China and India, and his European homeland. He had never gotten any closer to Asia than he had in his youth. At that point he served on a ship to

Khios in what is today, Greece. His persistence in pursuing the funding for such a great endeavor met strong resistance.

Several before him had set sail westward only to never return again, and the royal court advisors on such matters blocked his every effort wherever he was granted an audience. From Portugal to Genoa, on to Greece and, eventually, to Spain, he was denied the funding and provisions necessary to conduct such an uncertain venture. His first audience before Queen Isabella and King Ferdinand II was not exceptionally successful. The presentation was passed along to royal advisors on the subject, and after nearly two years of deliberation, it was determined that he had grossly underestimated the distance from Spain to his projected destination. The monarchs, however, did not want to allow him to proceed to other potential sponsors. They gave him an annual stipend and a letter to any city in their realm he traveled to provide him free food and shelter.

Columbus refused to be denied, and after about two years of staying the course and lobbying, he convinced the crown to sponsor his venture. It helped that the kingdom had just ended a war it had been involved in for many years. This apparently opened up the coffers to invest in a more risky venture. He was certain his was the right plan. And his reward was to be designated Admiral of the Open Sea and Governor of any lands he would claim in the name of Spain.

The course he presented was a new approach never before attempted. He had decided to travel southward first to the Canary Islands just off the northwest coast of mainland Africa. From there he would catch the strong westerly flow of the

Atlantic and sail the brisk winds that moved the same direction. Once he reached his goal, he would travel northward and follow the returning wind and sea currents homeward.

Many would stop here and believe that the only passion which drove Columbus was to travel the globe and find the quickest route of trade available. Recent history focuses on the greed aspect, and the belief that Columbus was a man who wanted only the fame and accolades that come with being one of extreme wealth and a successful explorer. One would be led from this view to believe that he completely overlooked the value of mankind in conquest of his desires.

Was he perfect? No. Yet in God's plan for the world He has more often than not used those we would consider severely flawed. Moses was a murderer. King David was an adulterer who had his lover's husband killed so he could cover the truth of his illegitimate child. Samson was overcome by his earthly desires. While Columbus may not be the subject of biblical matter, he was someone whose worldview projected a desire to proclaim the message of Christ.

Columbus himself saw his accomplishments primarily in the light of the spreading of the Christian religion.[1] Before they were "accomplishments" they were dreams. His journal entries throughout the voyage westward depicted his unwavering focus to reach Asia and to bring his faith to that region. His prologue to journal entries set out the purpose of the voyage quite clearly.

---

[1] Christopher Columbus Encyclopædia Britannica. 2013. *Encyclopædia Britannica Online*. 11 June 2013.

IN THE NAME OF OUR LORD JESUS CHRIST

BECAUSE, O most Christian, and very high, very excellent, and puissant Princes, King and Queen of the Spains and of the islands of the Sea, our Lords, in this present year of 1492, after your Highnesses had given an end to the war with the Moors who reigned in Europe, and had finished it in the very great city of Granada, where in this present year, on the second day of the month of January, by force of arms, I saw the royal banners of your Highnesses placed on the towers of Alhambra, which is the fortress of that city, and I saw the Moorish King come forth from the gates of the city and kiss the royal hands of your Highnesses, and of the Prince my Lord, and presently in that same month, acting on the information that I had given to your Highnesses touching the land of India... YOUR HIGHNESSES, as Catholic Christians And Princes who love the holy Christian faith; and the propagation of it, and who are enemies to the sect of Mahoma and to all idolatries and heresies, resolved to send me, Cristóbal Colon, to the said parts of India to see the said princes, and the cities and lands, and their disposition, with a view that they might be converted to our holy faith; and ordered that I should not go by land to the eastward; as had been customary, but that I should go by way of the west, whither up to this day, we do not know for certain that any one; has gone.[2]

---

[2] Original Source: Christopher Columbus, "Journal of the First Voyage of Columbus," in Julius E. Olson and Edward Gaylord Bourne, eds.,

Once reaching the islands, he wrote of the possibilities available for conversion of the natives. While some would try and insist that Columbus' intentions were solely focused on slavery, it is clear that he had a spiritual cause in mind.

> Presently many inhabitants of the island assembled. What follows is in the actual words of the Admiral in his book of the first navigation and discovery of the Indies. "I," he says, "that we might form great friendship, for I knew that they were a people who could be more easily freed and converted to our holy faith by love than by force, gave to some of them red caps, and glass beads to put round their necks, and many other things of little value, which gave them great pleasure, and made them so much our friends that it was a marvel to see... They should be good servants and intelligent, for I observed that they quickly took in what was said to them, and I believe that they would easily be made Christians, as it appeared to me that they had no religion. I, our Lord being pleased, will take hence, at the time of my departure, six natives for your Highnesses, that they may learn to speak. (12 October 1492)[3]

While Columbus did see these natives as potential servants, it was their gentle nature that he saw as open to the Christian faith. It is very clear in his writings that his intentions were to spread God's Word to the far reaches of the world. He was flawed

---

The Northmen, Columbus and Cabot, 985-1503, Original Narratives of Early American History. New York: Charles Scribner's Sons, 1906.
[3]   Ibid

6

in some of his approaches, and his leadership was less than desirable, as indicated in the complaints received by the Crown regarding his 'governorship' over the new settlements. But in the overall perspective of Columbus' voyages, Christianity was a prominent force pressing his exploration across the waves.

Over the next several decades, Spanish explorers and settlers traveled to the New World bringing with them Priests to establish worship centers for use in converting the native population. In Central and South America, as well as the Caribbean and southern North America, the growth of Spanish influence gave a vehicle for the continuance of the spread of the gospel of Christ into "all the world."

In just a few short years after the initial voyage of Columbus, more countries joined in commissioning expeditions across the ocean. While Spain and Portugal were progressing in their intentions to colonize what is now known as South America, the English ventured to launch to attempt a pathway north. The fleets of Spain and Portugal controlled the seas toward the south, and were powerful enough to defend the territory they perceived as their own.

In 1497, just five short years after Columbus' adventure across the Atlantic, John Cabot was commissioned by the English Crown to see if a "Northwest Passage" was available to the Orient. The documents or "patents" given to him indicated that he was granted permission to explore and establish claim to any lands found amongst the heathen in the name of the nation and Christianity. These are the same commissions granted to further explorers who launched under the same banner.

Several attempts to press into the heartland of North America and locate a direct route to China were made: each with the understanding that it was under authority of God and country.

Within the next several decades, the English laid claim to much of the North American Continent through multiple excursions to locate the every elusive passage to the riches of Asia. It was eventually discovered that the great navigators of the open ocean had, indeed, located a new land full of mineral wealth of its own. The edicts of the European monarchs were all similar: post the banner of the kingdom and establish the Christian faith among the heathen natives.

It was not long before the various nations of the European continent set out to establish a permanent presence in America. The now infamous Roanoke colony was England's first such attempt. Queen Elizabeth I, also known as "the Virgin Queen", gave Sir Walter Raleigh a charter to explore and settle the lands of North America in the authority of England:

ELIZABETH by the Grace of God of England, France and Ireland Queen, defender of the faith, &c. To all people to whom these presents shall come, greeting.

Know ye that of our especial grace, certain science, and mere motion, we have given and granted, and by these presents for us, our heirs and successors, we give and grant to our trustee and well beloved servant *Walter Raleigh*, Esquire, and to his heirs assignee for ever, free liberty and license from time to time, and at all times for ever hereafter, to discover, search, find out, and view such remote, heathen and barbarous lands, countries, and territories, not actually possessed of any Christian Prince, nor inhabited by Christian People, as to him, his heirs and assignee, and to every or any of them shall seem good...

*　　*　　*

...for as much as upon the finding out, discovering, or inhabiting of such remote lands, countries, and territories as aforesaid, it shall be necessary for the safety of all men, that shall adventure themselves in those journeys or voyages, to determine to live together in Christian peace, and civil quietness each with other, whereby every one may with snore pleasure and profit enjoy that whereunto they shall attain with great Paine and peril... [4]

It was clearly established that Raleigh, and those he would assign to do so, should qualify any lands they found for exploration and claim to be those not already claimed by *Christian* people. In most of the grants and charters given during this time the monarch executing such determined their actions to be those in representation of the country and Christianity.

On April 27, 1584, Raleigh sent two captains across the Atlantic to locate a suitable area for a permanent colony. July 4th, while

---

[4]　The Federal and State Constitutions Colonial Charters, and Other Organic Laws of the States, Territories, and Colonies Now or Heretofore Forming the United States of America. Compiled and Edited Under the Act of Congress of June 30, 1906 by Francis Newton Thorpe Washington, DC : Government Printing Office, 1909. (Olde English words rewritten into contemporary English by Rexford Louth, Author)

exploring the coast, they came upon Roanoke Island. This was decided to be the setting for the attempt. Commissioned by the mandate set forth, a group of settlers set sail in April, 1585 under the command of Sir Richard Greenville.

The fleet finally reached Roanoke Island in July, after a detour to Puerto Rico. A storm had separated one of the five ships from the other and they regrouped as agreed upon before setting sail. Now at their destination, the establishment of the colony was underway.

Over the next two years attempts to settle the area were troubled, to say the least. The result of the effort was tragic. When a relief ship returned to bring assistance to the second group of colonists in August of 1590, it was found that all of them were missing. The ninety men, seventeen women, and eleven children, including the first English child born in America, Virginia Dare, had vanished without a trace.

*   *   *

The first successful attempt at settlement of the New World by the English was under the charter granted by King James I of England, Scotland, and Ireland. Jamestown, named so in honor of the king, was established in May, 1607. The fleet had arrived two weeks prior, and had explored the Virginia coastline until the location deemed best suited for success was found. The ships anchored May 13th, and the men disembarked and began building the structures the following day.

The charter gave the Virginia Company of London the authority to set up permanent colonies for England. Specifically, it gave set instruction for the establishment of two such colonies segmented by latitudes along the coastline. It was very sure in stating that they were not to pursue this attempt anywhere "which are... now actually possessed by any Christian Prince or People."[5]

Furthermore, King James I, who also set forth the development of the "King James Bible", laid out the purpose for such exploration and colonization:

> We, greatly commending, and graciously accepting of, their Desires for the Furtherance of so noble a Work, which may, by the Providence of Almighty God, hereafter tend to the Glory of his Divine Majesty, in propagating of Christian Religion to such People, as yet live in Darkness and miserable Ignorance of the true Knowledge and Worship of God, and may in time bring the Infidels and Savages, living in those parts, to human Civility, and to a settled and quiet Government: DO, by these our Letters Patents, graciously accept of, and agree to, their humble and well-intended Desires;... [6]

The turbulent years ahead would see the group face times of great famine, attacks by tribes of native Americans, and harsh winters. Some would even resort to cannibalism in the worse

---

[5] The Federal and State Constitutions Colonial Charters, and Other Organic Laws of the States, Territories, and Colonies Now or Heretofore Forming the United States of America. Compiled and Edited Under the Act of Congress of June 30, 1906 by Francis Newton Thorpe Washington, DC : Government Printing Office, 1909.

[6] Ibid

time of starvation. Yet through all these things, persistence paid off. The arrival of a second group of settlers in June, 1610, along with the marriage of John Rolfe to the native Chief Powhatan's daughter, Pocahontas gave the colony the strength it needed to firmly anchor the settlement into the decades ahead.

While the struggle to maintain the settlement did not end there for the inhabitants of Jamestown, these two events laid the much needed foundation to the fledgling group.

A short time later, in 1619, the first representative government in America came into existence at the colony. On July 30, 1619, the group convened for a six-day meeting at the church on Jamestown Island, Virginia. A council chosen by the Virginia Company as advisers to the governor, the Virginia Governor's counsel, met as an "upper house," while twenty-two elected representatives met as the House of Burgesses. Together, the House of Burgesses and the Council would be the Virginia General Assembly.[7] Two representatives were to be chosen from their respective "Plantation freely to be elected by the inhabitants thereof."

Initially, the two houses were not separate, but met together. Before the first session commenced the body made their first, and perhaps most important, decision.

According the transcript of the meeting, "…for as muche as mens affaires doe little prosper where Gods service is neglected; all

---

[7]   Rubin, Jr. Louis D. *Virginia: A History.*New York W.W. Norton & Company, Inc., 1977. pp. 3–27.

the Burgesses took their places in the Quire, till a Prayer was said by Mr *Bucke*, the Minister, that it would please God to guide us & sanctifie all our proceedings to his owne glory, and the good of his Plantation."[8] It is then noted that once Prayer was concluded, they began the proceedings having obtained God's blessing.

This legislature continued and eventually progressed to become the House of Senate and House of Delegates formulated in Virginia's Constitution of 1776. The House of Burgesses had been officially dissolved in 1774 due to the colony's support of resistance to the Crown, but continued to meet discreetly. It is noteworthy that such names as George Washington, Thomas Jefferson, and Patrick Henry, among others, were trained initially in this legislative body.

While the Jamestown settlement was underway, a group of Pilgrims seeking religious freedom from the laws forbidding independent worship outside the Church of England were preparing themselves for a colonization effort of their own. The 1559 Act of Uniformity had declared any who opposed the Church given authority by the English Crown to be imprisoned and heavily fined. Even those not attending "authorized" services were fined for each Sunday and "holy day" they missed attendance. The group originally petitioned to be allowed to meet outside the Church of England, and be given the ability to conduct their services as they saw fit.

---

[8] Transcription Source: H. R. McIlwaine, ed., *Journals of the House of Burgesses, 1619–1658/59* (Richmond: Virginia State Library, 1915), 4.

The only thing requested from the Puritans that was granted by King James was an English translation of the Bible. Again, this is the same King James Bible widely accepted throughout Christianity. In the years following, William Bradford, a member of the congregation, wrote in his journal, "...they could not long continue in any peaceable condition, but were hunted & persecuted on every side..."[9] Seeing that their efforts were being denied and the struggle growing worse and worse, the congregation decided to move to the neutral ground of Amsterdam.

Before long the group realized that their children, and thus their society, were losing their identity. Their young people came under the liberal influence of the society where they had fled to seek refuge. They were Englishmen.

The decision to move was not an easy one, but they chose to brave the elements involved rather than lose their children to the ungodly influences around them. In addition to avoiding the loss of their youth, Bradford indicates that there was a "...great hope, for the propagating and advancing the gospel of the kingdom of Christ in those remote parts of the world."[10]

Once the choice had been made, ambassadors representing the Puritans traveled to England to seek hope in relocating

---

[9] Bradford, William (1898) [1651]. Hildebrandt, Ted, ed. *Bradford's History "Of Plimoth Plantation"* Boston: Wright & Potter Printing Co. , Book 1, Chapter 1

[10] Bradford, William (1898) [1651]. Hildebrandt, Ted, ed. *Bradford's History "Of Plimoth Plantation"* Boston: Wright & Potter Printing Co. , Book 1, Chapter 4

under English rule to America. They approached The London Company (The Virginia Company of London, as previously noted), the group holding considerable land area under the charters granted them, to seek an area close enough to Jamestown for protection, yet far enough away as not to allow undue influence from the Church of England. The King ultimately agreed to such a colonization effort with the understanding that their religious practices would not receive official connotation by the Crown.

After several failed attempts to launch toward America in two ships, the smaller *Speedwell,* and the larger *Mayflower,* the lesser ship was deemed unseaworthy. As a result, a lesser number of the crew and passengers were consolidated onto the *Mayflower.* This now infamous ship set sail on September 16, 1620 by the modern calendar. The passengers and crew were now comprised of both those placed aboard by the investors of The London Company as well as the young members of the congregation. At a point more than halfway to the New World, strong winds caused a main beam to crack. It was considered to return to England, but the crew was able to repair the beam sufficiently to complete the voyage by what is believed to be a large clamp brought along by the colonists to assist in house construction.

The arrival at their new home brought great joy. It was late in the year, and enduring the contrary seas had worn on the entire group. They had tried to travel further inland, but were unable to navigate into the mouth of the river. This spot was to be home. William Brewster, pastor of the Puritan congregation, led the group in reciting Psalm 100 as a prayer of thanksgiving:

¹ Make a joyful noise unto the LORD, all ye lands.

² Serve the LORD with gladness: come before his presence with singing.

³ Know ye that the LORD he is God: it is he that hath made us, and not we ourselves; we are his people, and the sheep of his pasture.

⁴ Enter into his gates with thanksgiving, and into his courts with praise: be thankful unto him, and bless his name.

⁵ For the LORD is good; his mercy is everlasting; and his truth endureth to all generations.

A final charter had not been completed at the time of the voyage, and some among the group believed that they were not held accountable to the agreement they had in place. In order to accommodate the entire group, a contract which came to be known as the *Mayflower Compact* was adopted by a democratic process. This document established the first constitution in America. The following is known as the "modern" version of the original document, created by Steve Mount from the Olde English manuscripts:

In the name of God, Amen. We, whose names are underwritten, the Loyal Subjects of our dread Sovereign Lord King James, by the Grace of God, of Great Britain, France, and Ireland, King, defender of the Faith, etc.:

Having undertaken, for the Glory of God, and advancements of the Christian faith, and the honor of our King and Country, a voyage to plant the first colony in the Northern parts of Virginia; do by these presents, solemnly and mutually, in the presence of God, and one another; covenant and combine ourselves together into a civil body politic; for our better ordering, and preservation and furtherance of the ends aforesaid; and by virtue hereof to enact, constitute, and frame, such just and equal laws, ordinances, acts, constitutions, and offices, from time to time, as shall be thought most meet and convenient for the general good of the colony; unto which we promise all due submission and obedience.[11]

These brave men and women planted themselves in Plimouth, modern day Plymouth, in the territory which is today the State of Massachusetts. Again, as noted in this document, the emphasis was that this group had traveled across the many miles of open ocean, facing treacherous conditions, for the "Glory of God, and the advancements of the Christian faith", as well as for the kingdom from which they set sail.

The story of the Puritans, known to us as the Pilgrims, their survival and the great celebration of Thanksgiving upon overcoming the great odds against them, is legend. With the help of those Native Americans around them, they were granted favor from that divine Hand which would guide the course of this land for the many years to come. Today we carry on the tradition of giving thanks to God for His grace shed on us.

---

[11]   http://www.usconstitution.net/mayflower.html

With both the two-house legislature established in Jamestown, and those of central Virginia, and the democratic process set forth in Plymouth, the idea of a government of representation was laid out in the minds of these colonists. Both were here in the name of God. All had come with the purpose of being free to conduct themselves as God led them.

Yes, as many have pointed out, the surge toward American colonization was not all for the "glory of God". Much emphasis was placed on securing the land and its resources. It was presented to the rulers of Europe that there was gold, a precious commodity, encased in the region. The time of expansion across the ocean brought many who were determined to obtain personal gain. Fame and fortune lured those craving such things. However, when viewed in the light of the grand design of Providence, these were a distant second to developing a land that would ultimately reach back across the entire globe with the gospel of Jesus Christ.

Colonial Christianity

Take just a moment and imagine yourself on the deck of a sailing vessel of old. Forget for a moment that you have probably been trapped on this ship with 120 of your closest acquaintances under some of the most repulsive conditions for nearly two months with nary a change of clothing.

Take a step forward toward the railing and feel the ocean breeze as the mist rushes across your face. Taste the bit of salt as that same mist gathers on your lips. And suddenly there on the horizon appears a most welcome sight: the shoreline of your new home. Whether it is a sandy beach or a rocky inlet, you have arrived at your destination. You may be quite apprehensive since the known landscape of your European homeland lies over a thousand miles away, and what lies ahead is uncertainly and unfamiliar territory. It is said to be an untamed land, and savage in some respects. But now it is home.

As you look around you see the great masts rising from the deck, weathered and aged with time and the elements. Above, the billowing white sails are fully extended by the winds which carry you along. The sounds of orders are engulfing the deck as the crew heeds the voices of their superiors.

Soon the ship slows in anticipation of anchoring for the initial disembarking. Before long, you are gathering with your family into the boat that will take you ashore. Stepping somewhat timidly onto the foreign soil you take your first few steps onto a land you are about to become intimately familiar with. You scan the obstacles and opportunities that will allow you to formulate your future. You are in America.

For thousands of colonists this is how it was for them. Uncertainties abounded as to where they would set up their home and how all of their activities would come together to create the familiarity of what is theirs. The structures began to take shape and neighbors were established. Communities formed in a bond that became more than just an existence near one another. In many instances one's very survival depended on knowing you could count on those around you.

We have already taken a brief look at the Puritans and their quest for religious freedom to serve God as they saw fit. They were known to strictly enforce their beliefs on any who dwelt in their territory. Local governments, and thereby local laws, caused some to be imprisoned, physically punished, and seriously fined for not following the creeds set forth.

These Puritans began to lose their hold on the ability to enforce such edicts, and by the middle of the 17th Century many had heard the call to come and serve the Almighty as they saw fit on the newly found continent. The colonial identity was one of common faith in Christianity with diversified approaches. For quite some time this worked for the benefit of both the Crown and the settlers. The kingdom of England was able to establish footholds in America while those wishing for the freedom to pursue their love for God as they would had open reign to do so.

In the mid 17th Century a group of religious followers of Christ began to formulate around the idea of serving a sovereign God. They believed that God wished a believer to acknowledge Him in sincere reverence. They came to be known as Quakers, derived from the belief that they were to "tremble in the way of the Lord". The official title of the group was the Religious Society of Friends.

One of their key ideals was that they insisted that God could speak to the common man without intervention by members of the clergy. They believed that no one had to be trained in seminary in order to be able to ascend the pulpit. They strongly felt that the concept of tithe had been manipulated into a means of control and further taxation by the organized Church of England with the blessing of the monarchy. Their worship services were primarily places of quiet *waiting* for the Spirit of God.

Another focal point of their faith stated that the women of Christianity were on equal ground as the men. This was, as you may well imagine, quite popular with many ladies during the time of the gathering's formation. One of the roles granted to women in the movement was that of having major roles in the marriage ceremony. This particular wedge drove many who were marginal in their Quaker beliefs away from the congregation.

With these concepts you may think they were more liberal in their thinking regarding the Christian's conduct. The truth is that they were driven to be a bit more restrictive on many issues due to their severe respect for the fact that God was, in fact, GOD. One was to conduct themselves in "fear and trembling, in singleness of heart, as unto Christ." (Ephesians 6:5)

They came under serious attack by those of the sanctioned Church of England. Their conduct had come under scrutiny by the watchful eyes of those in authority of the religious theocracy. Their leader, George Fox, was imprisoned off and on throughout two decades of his life for his teaching. Their refusal to bow to any civil authority, or to swear allegiance to any government brought intensive persecution on those who strictly adhered to their belief system.

Seeking refuge as the Puritans had, many Quakers moved to the Netherlands, a place they believed to be neutral in religious practice. Within a few short years it was observed by visitors to the region that the persecution in the area had grown as severe as that they had endured in England.

About this time, William Penn, friends with the English Crown, had been rumored to pen a document for King James II of

England granting lenience to those of religious beliefs not aligning with the Church of England. This, however, did not last, and William Penn secured a charter to settle the area now known as Pennsylvania, or "Penn's Woods" from King Charles II. This effort by Penn was known as the "Holy Experiment", joining together both the earthly and the spiritual.

While those of the Dutch religious community did not completely align with the ways of the Quakers, the persecution both faced caused an alliance. These joined forces to move to the New World with the promise of the elimination of persecution. Travel by the end of the 17th Century had grown more common, and the combined congregation moved swiftly to set up their homesteads in the chartered areas. The capital of the land would be called Philadelphia, or, "the City of Brotherly Love".

The tremendous drawing power of the new colony was the guarantee of religious freedom. This edict was strictly adhered to. Knowing they had the ability to serve God in their own fashion lured many of various faiths to the land. The colonial expansion was impressive over the next few decades as those seeking freedom funneled in. By the early 18th Century the colony was thriving.

One problem arose, however, as the Quakers were not by practice endeared to government. The colony had to have a rule of law, and the Quakers stepped away from such for the most part, allowing those more inclined to step in and have rule over the territory.

The Quakers had originally held to the ability to own slaves as long as those masters properly provided for the nurturing of soul, mind and body. However, by the mid 18th Century almost all Quakers had moved toward abolition. At that time only about 10% of Quaker households had slaves.

Quakers also began migrating across the new colonies, carrying their message of true faith in Christ as they went their ways. Severe persecution of the group occurred in the Puritan stronghold of Massachusetts. The Puritans had developed a practice of their own in government and worship, the only accepted religious practice was theirs.

In the final decade of the 17th Century, however, the English government pressed upon the Puritans the need to lax their strangle hold on observances. With greater government influence from across the ocean, the need to adhere to the *English Toleration Act of 1689* forced its way upon them. Though not pleased with having to do so, they found themselves unable to push back against the insistence of the King.

Because of the widespread laxness of control upon the congregants, a more secular view of life arose. Many ministers of the early 18th Century grew more and more concerned that the youth of the congregation, especially, were being drawn toward lifestyles displeasing to God. They were pointing out that such things as earthquakes, debilitating diseases, and even Native American uprisings were the results of God's wrath.

Almost simultaneously, the Holy Spirit had captured the hearts of some young ministers in proclaiming the need for a revival in the colonies. These evangelists came under intense ridicule because they did not arise from the traditional pulpit processes, but had been implanted with an urgency to present the Word of God in a fiery way, bringing many to repent and come to Christ.

Men such as Gilbert Tennent, and later, Jonathan Edwards, traveled the countryside warning of the hell which awaits those who refuse to keep themselves in the service of Jesus Christ. And then came George Whitefield.

George Whitefield, a proselyte of Charles and John Wesley while attending Pembroke College in Oxford, England, had experienced the "new birth" while there, and felt compelled to take his message across the Atlantic to the New Georgia colony. He spent a bit of time beforehand in London, expressing the Gospel in a way none could recall before. His outward demonstrations brought the characters and concepts of the Bible to life. He did make it to Georgia, but stayed only three months.

After returning to England, he found that many were now resistant to his message. Compelled again to travel to America, he arrived in the New England colonies in 1739 and began a two year crusade up and down the coast. His first stop, Philadelphia, found 8,000 colonists who attended. There was no church that could handle such audiences, so the ministry was taken outside.

Everywhere he traveled the results were the same: Overwhelming crowds gathered to hear the message. While his was a more gracious message than that of Edwards, the element of eternal damnation for those unwilling to yield themselves to the service of a loving Christ who had given Himself on the cross for their sin still prevailed. Whitefield delivered a message in Philadelphia on August 24, 1746. In the sermon, titled *Unnatural Rebellion,* he brought attention to I Corinthians 13 in which Paul insists that all the service one may engage in, though necessary to please God, is worthless without love.

At the zenith of The Great Awakening, Jonathan Edwards delivered what was, perhaps, his most powerful and compelling message, *Sinners in the Hand of an Angry God,* at Enfield, Massachusetts. Through those 'native' to the colonies, and the ministry of George Whitefield, driven to New England to present an impassioned Gospel, thousands came to know Christ as their personal Savior.

The period from the mid 17th Century to the mid 18th Century had brought an abundance of Christianity in multiple forms to the shores of America. Catholics and Protestants, alike, established centers for worship as they chose to worship the one true Almighty God. From the liturgical to the conventional, and onward to the radical, each pocket of the Christian faith promoted Jesus Christ as Lord.

Beginning in 1654, at the seaport town of New Amsterdam, which would one day become the City of New York, Jewish refugees seeking freedom of religious worship settled into the New World. Thriving communities sprung up along the coast giving America the reputation of true freedom of religion. Synagogues began to be found throughout New England.

The Judeo-Christian faith in God now had a stronghold in America. Strong seminaries arose in which many were taught God's Word even while pursuing other careers. Great leaders arising in the various aspects of colonial life that would eventually facilitate movements toward the Declaration of Independence some decades later were trained in the essential knowledge of the Christian faith.

The first colleges, not including pre-collegiate academies, were: Harvard in Massachusetts (1636); the College of William and Mary in Virginia (1693); Yale (1701), the College of New Jersey (subsequently Princeton) (1746); King's College (subsequently Columbia) New York, (1754); the College of Philadelphia (subsequently the University of Pennsylvania) (1755); and Queen's College in New Jersey (subsequently Rutgers) (1766).[12]

John Adams completed an education at Harvard, the University in Boston, near his home town of Braintree. Thomas Jefferson attended the College of William and Mary. Most of the time, the college president would be a member of the clergy. The reason most of the schools were instituted was to prepare young men (only white males were admitted at the time) for integrating religion and societal processes in order that they might be able to be strong citizens.

Contrary to what has been put forth in recent years, religious practice throughout the American colonies in the 18th Century

---

[12] Wikimedia Foundation, Wikipedia-The Free Encyclopedia, *Education in the Thirteen Colonies.* Last modified July 9, 2013, http://en.wikipedia. org/wiki/Education_in_the_Thirteen_Colonies [accessed July 9, 2013]

was on the rise. Many "scholars" have attempted to rewrite America's history to state that those who are well known in the formation of the United States of America were either atheists or deists. We will deal with those untruths later.

Proof of the persistent impression of Christian faith during the 17th and 18th Centuries is a small book prepared for distribution among young students throughout the colonies. This book, *The New England Primer*, was not only a "best seller" during the century it was primarily used from 1690 through 1790, but it was *the* textbook, next to the Bible itself, that was to be used in sanctioned schools.

This was first published in the New World by Benjamin Harrison, who had published the basic book under the name *The Protestant Tutor*, in England. This text was only replaced by the appearance of Noah Webster's *Blue Back Speller*, which taught similar principles.

The *New England Primer* taught the young their ABCs by using many lessons from the Bible. The associated words taken from the King James Bible were presented with a small woodcut picture to the left, and a memorization rhyme to the right. Some examples are "**P**eter denies, His Lord, and cries", "**Q**ueen Esther comes in royal state, To save the Jews from dismal fate", "**R**achel doth mourn, For her first born", "**S**amuel anoints, Whom God appoints", "**T**ime cuts down all, Both great and small", and "**U**riah's lovely wife, Made David seek his life."[13]

---

[13]   Ford, Paul Leicester. *The New-England Primer* (NY, 1899)

In addition to the basic spelling principles, the book also tutored on key elements of the Christian faith. The colonial version of this book presented these truths with more relevant items from life in America as well. One section of the book deals with one's approach to the Lord's Prayer.

Q. 98. *What is prayer?*

A. Prayer is an offering up of our desires to God for things agreeable to his will, in the name of Christ, with confession of our sins, & thankful acknowledgement of his mercies.

Q. 99. *What rule hath God given us for our direction in prayer?*

A. The whole word of God is of use to direct us but the special rule of direction is that form of prayer which Christ taught his disciples commonly called, *The Lord's Prayer.*

Q. 100 *What doth the preface of the Lord's prayer teach us?*

A. The preface of the Lord's prayer which is *Our Father which art in heaven,* teacheth us, to draw near to God with all holy reverence and confidence, as children to a father, able and ready to help us, and that we should pray with and for others.[14]

---

[14]   Ibid

The following questions and answers dissect the elements of *The Lord's Prayer.* Immediately after this particular group of questions came, in later texts, an area called *SPIRITUAL MILK for American BABES.* This dealt with truths taken, as it clearly states, from "both testaments". The following is a sample that begins that section.

Q. *What hath God done for you?*

A. God hath made me, he keepeth me, and he can save me.

Q. *What is God?*

A. God is a Spirit of himself and for himself.

Q. *How many Gods be there?*

A. There is but one God in three Persons, the Father, and the Son, and the Holy Ghost.[15]

And this began the spiritual lessons children, whom we would classify as elementary school age, were taught and expected to know. These lessons were continuously reviewed until such a time as the child would be able to recite the appropriate answer.

As I reviewed the book, nearly 90 pages long, I was amazed at the depth of some of the questions. To my knowledge, there are many within Christianity today who may not be able

---

15   Ford, Paul Leicester. *The New-England Primer* (NY, 1899)

to adequately answer some of the more powerful questions presented to these very young people.

Q. 21. *Who is the Redeemer of God's elect?*

A. The only Redeemer of God's elect, is the Lord Jesus Christ, who being the eternal Son of God, became man, and so was, and continues to be, God and man, in two distinct natures, and one person forever.

Q. 22. *How did Christ being the Son of God become man?*

A. Christ the Son of God became man by taking to himself a true body and a reasonable soul, being conceived by the power of the Holy Ghost, in the womb of the virgin Mary, and born of her, and yet without sin.

Q. 23. *What offices doth Christ execute as our Redeemer?*

A. Christ as our Redeemer executes the office of a prophet, of a priest, & of a king, both in his estate of humiliation and exaltation.[16]

The questions that follow in numbers twenty-four and beyond would be embarrassing to many, asking how Christ executes His office of prophet (24), priest (25), and king (26). They are further asked what the meaning and impact his humiliation, exaltation, and so forth have on the process of Christian faith.

---

[16]   Ibid

It is apparent that the great majority of the families in New England in the 18th Century were intent on their children being grounded in the truths of God's Word. While the "Age of Reason" so many talk about arose during this time, and some of the very tenants of the faith were debated, the greater number of colonists followed the one, true God, with Christianity at the very center of the average family's existence.

In fact, according to the Library of Congress' website:

> Against a prevailing view that eighteenth-century Americans had not perpetrated the first settlers' passionate commitment to their faith, scholars now identify a high level of religious energy in colonies after 1700. According to one expert, religion was in the "ascension rather than declension"; another sees a "rising vitality in religious life" from 1700 onward; and a third finds religion in many parts of the colonies in a state of "feverish growth." Figures on church attendance and church formation support these opinions. Between 1700 and 1740, and estimated 75 to 80 percent of the population attended churches, which were being built at a headlong pace.[17]

During this time of religious revival those churches which were accepting and promoting the "new birth" being presented by George Whitefield began to thrive. While retaining their

---

[17]   [6] United States of America, Library of Congress, *Religion and the Founding of the American Republic, II. Religion in Eighteenth-Century America.* Last modified July 23, 2010, http://www.loc.gov/exhibits/religion/rel02.html [accessed July 12, 2013]

separate congregational identities, the Baptists, Methodists, and Presbyterians developed a cooperative of ministry in outreach to the colonies. Pulpits, revitalized by the fresh breeze of the movement of the Holy Ghost, thundered the gospel each week to congregations hungry for the Word.

One such sermon was presented by Rev. Charles Chauncy, DD, one of the Pastors of the First Church in Boston on May 27, 1747. This was given before William Shirley, Esq, governor and counsel to King George II of England; and the House of Representatives of the Providence of the Massachusetts-Bay in New England in advance of the legislative session they were about to conduct. The message was based on II Samuel 23:3, "The God of Israel said, the Rock of Israel spake to me; he that ruleth over Men must be just, ruling in the Fear of God." This is the exact reference as inscribed by Rev. Chauncy at the beginning of his text.

Over the next hour, the pastor proceeded to instruct the governor and representatives on what it truly means to rule in a "just" manor. He began by pointing out the instruction by God to the kings of Israel, and how that directly related to their roles in particular. He stated clearly that there is a "certain order among men, according to which some are entrusted with power to rule over others."[18] The pastor further instructs that, "They must be just. They ought to be so in their private capacity; maintaining a care to exhibit in their conduct towards all they are concerned with, a fair transcript of that fundamental law of the religion of

---

[18]   Sandoz, Ellis, ed. 1991 *Political Sermons of the American Founding Era: 1730-1805*. Indianapolis: Liberty Fund p.142

Jesus, as well as eternal rule of natural justice..."[19] It is clear
that he felt no difficulty in addressing the need for Christian
leadership.

In all, the message covered such topics as being just in the
use of their power, adhering to the limitations granted by
the constitution under which they are appointed or elected;
just related to the laws by which they govern, not allowing
themselves to be swayed by "biass, either from self-will, or self-
interest; the smiles or frowns of men greater than themselves;
or the humour of the populace"[20]; and that they must always
keep in mind that the sovereign eternal judge, King of Kings, is
ever mindful of their proceedings.

Even subjects such as proper taxation measures and amounts
were covered, acknowledging the necessity of governments
to gather support from the populace to sustain its operations
and employ its leadership. Strong warning against becoming
gluttonous with greed was given also. He instructed them in
being wary of making decisions "under the influence of worldly
views and selfish designs."[21] He warned that, "The natural
effect whereof must be the ruin of a people."[22]

The Reverend did recognize that one was not required to be
Christian in order to serve well in capacities of a government
office. He pointedly addressed this topic by saying that there are

---

[19] Sandoz, Ellis, ed. 1991 *Political Sermons of the American Founding
Era: 1730-1805.* Indianapolis: Liberty Fund, p.145
[20] Ibid, p.148
[21] Ibid, p.165
[22] Ibid, p.165

those who may be able to conduct themselves justly by a self-produced sense of morality. The great concern he promoted was that without Jesus Christ as one's Lord and Savior the person may find it quite difficult to avoid the temptations of greed and corruption that would naturally face them in their positions.

A general observation from his study of scripture was that all they did in their roles in government was to be "done under the guidance of an habitual awe of God, a serious regard to his governing will, and their accountableness to him."[23] His conclusion, which carried on for several minutes, was labeled *APPLICATION* and outlined the specific actions suggested for the magistrate and those serving in the House.

It was in this crucible of Christian passion that young men were growing to become the leaders of the greatest nation on the earth. It was the fires of the gospel that ignited within these pliable hearts the desire to live truly free. And it was sermons such as that reviewed above that pressed upon them what to look for in their monarch, governors, and those in positions of ruling over them.

Those threatened by the facts of Christianity at the very foundations of American life and the development of the documents which placed the United States of America officially on the map will fight with every ounce of their strength to disprove such to be true. I am convinced that there is a very strong underlying principle that drives their assault against

---

[23]   Ibid, p.166

Christianity in general, and its influence on American formulation and society. This principle is merely that a Christian foundation means there is a precedent to employ righteousness in government, and that would require one to consider that God is at the very center of not only the nation, but the entire universe. This means they may very well stand before the ultimate Judge of mankind one day; and that eats at their very soul, exposing a gap they cannot fill without the Lord.

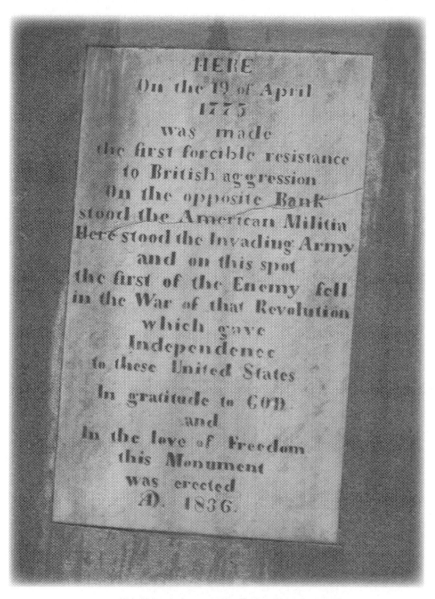

PLACARD COMMEMORATING THE
BATTLE OF CONCORD
"The shot heard round the world"
Concord, Massachusettes

Faith and Freedom

There was a great stirring that had arisen in the colonies of New England which transformed them from loyal servants into a nation striving for independence. A message had been sounded from one end of the land to the other, and it was a very clear voice. The group sounding the call to freedom was probably one that was unexpected.

Insight to the contempt held toward this group may be found in an article written by Tory Peter Oliver entitled *Origin and Process of the American Rebellion*. He first begins to organize his argument against the Colonies by introducing what he believes to be an argument against the need for such *rebellion* based on their status as a *nurtured* land under the gentle graces of a compassionate monarchy. He then begins the assault against their churches, blaming the clergy for augmenting the rebellion.

They have a Religion of their own, which, to the eternal Disgrace of many Nations, who boast of Politeness, is more influential on their Conduct than that of those who hold them in so great contempt. As in the earliest Ages of the World, so among those Tribes, they adhere to Tradition for their Conduct, in the more important Scenes of Life.[24]

His course is set on the arguments levied against the pastors he perceives as despised perpetrators of sedition. They have, as he mentions above, devised a religion of their own based on traditions he calls unsubstantiated by the Bible. In the section of his 'letter' deemed "The Black Regiment", also termed "The Black Robe Regiment", derogatory terms he attached to the clergy supporting the revolution, he continues his expression of disgust. He speaks of "Mr. Otis's Black Regiment, the dissenting Clergy, who took so active a Part in the Rebellion."[25] And his anger continues as he describes the pulpits by saying, "they have been unceasingly sounding the Yell of Rebellion in the Ears of an ignorant & deluded People."[26]

In his discourse Oliver states, "The Clergy of this Province were, in general, a Set of very weak Men."[27] He proceeded to speculate that these men, leading congregations of commoner colonials, were being influenced by the fact that the people wanted to hear this message. Since these men drew their livelihood from the

---

[24] Adair, Douglass and John A. Schultz, eds. 1967 *Peter Oliver's Origin and Progress of the American Rebellion: A Tory View.* Stanford, California: Stanford University Press, 1961.

[25] Ibid

[26] Ibid

[27] Ibid

coffers of the churches, they were inclined to give a message acceptable. In other words, he was accusing those members of the various groups to be those who would "not endure sound doctrine, but according to their own desires, *because* they have itching ears, they will heap up for themselves teachers;" (II Timothy 4:3) In his slanted opinion, they had gathered together men who would tell them what they wanted to hear.

As his letter continues, Judge Oliver, as he was appointed justice of the supreme court over the Massachusetts colony, begins to speak in particular about some of the ministers he has encountered in his time in New England. "Among those who were most distinguished of the Boston Clergy were Dr. Charles Chauncy, Dr. Jonathan Mayhew & Dr. Samuel Cooper; & they distinguished theirselves in encouraging seditions & Riots, until those lesser Offences were absorbed in Rebellion."[28]

His accusation that these were "very weak Men" appears very close to the scripture which states, "Now when they saw the boldness of Peter and John, and perceived that they were uneducated and untrained men, they marveled. And they realized that they had been with Jesus." (Acts 4:13) The arguments launched from the pulpits throughout New England were of the same nature: bold, and without apology.

Even King George III had come to look at one of the greatest problems of the "rebellion" as this "Black Robed Regiment". It was considered that the clergy were responding with anger

---

[28]   Ibid

at the suggestion from the Crown that each minister be duly licensed by the religious authorities of England.

As noted previously, Dr. Charles Chauncy was not slack in any way in approaching rightful legislation from a Christian perspective. His sermon entitled *Civil Magistrates Must Be Just, Ruling in the Fear of God* was covered in considerable length in the last chapter. Many other such messages were delivered by those named in Justice Oliver's accounting of the "rebellion", as well as from many unnamed.

One of the most powerful aspects of these messages went beyond the *thundering* of intensive voices in a passionate plea for righting the wrongs. This was the point of biblical authority. Sundays were filled with ministry which provided foundations for freedom from the very Word of God. The Bible was the text from which these in the Black Robe Regiment found their inspiration.

One of the most famous members of the Black Robe Regiment was Rev. Peter Muhlenberg. Pastor Muhlenberg was twice ordained: first in the Lutheran faith in 1768, and the second time while in England into the priesthood of the Anglican Church in 1772. He served a parish in New Jersey for five years and during that assignment married "Hannah" Meyer. It was while serving the Anglican congregation in Woodstock, Virginia that he began his defining ministry.

Much of his messages while in Virginia focused on the biblical evidences of true liberty. In just his second year of ministry as pastor there he was elected to the House of Burgesses. It was there that he came into contact with several patriots of the American Revolution, including George Washington who had been serving that body since 1758. The House of Burgesses also had membership during the tenure of Muhlenberg of such now-renown names as Thomas Jefferson (1768), Patrick Henry (1765) and Richard Henry Lee (1758), all whom had prominence in the advancement of the American Revolution.

The Second Continental Congress appointed George Washington as Commanding General of the freshly approved standing army of the colonies on June 15, 1775. Peter Muhlenberg, who had military experience by serving with the German dragoons while in Europe, was a natural selection to raise the 8th Virginia Regiment, and General Washington personally requested that he do so. Accepting the task, the newly appointed Colonel engaged in one of the most infamous actions accredited to the Black Robe Regiment.

There have been a few attempts of recent days to discredit the story which is related next; however, in examination of the texts closest to the event, there is strong evidence to its factual occurrence. In his book of 1849, *The Life of Major-General Peter Muhlenberg of the Revolutionary Army,* Henry Augustus Muhlenberg recounts the story based on the accounts of those living during the time.

> He [Peter Muhlenberg] was immediately commissioned, and proceeded to Dunmore to raise the regiment committed to his charge. Upon this occasion a well-authenticated anecdote is told of him, which gives us a deep insight into the character of the man, and the

feelings which induced him to abandon the altar for the sword. It shows of what sterling metal the patriots of olden time were formed.

*   *   *

Of the matter of the sermon various accounts remain. All concur, however, in attributing to it great potency in arousing the military ardour of the people, and unite in describing its conclusion. After recapitulating, in words that aroused the coldest, the story of their sufferings and their wrongs, and telling them of the sacred character of the struggle in which he had unsheathed his sword, and for which he had left the altar he had vowed to serve, he said "that, in the language of holy writ, there was a time for all things, a time to preach and a time to pray, but those times had passed away;" and in a voice that re-echoed through the church like a trumpet-blast, "that there was a time to fight, and that time had now come!"

The sermon finished, he pronounced the benediction. A breathless stillness brooded over the congregation. Deliberately putting off the gown, which had thus far covered his martial figure, he stood before them a girded warrior; and descending from the pulpit, ordered the drums at the church-door to beat for recruits. Then followed a scene to which even the American revolution, rich as it is in bright examples of the patriotic devotion of the people, affords no parallel. His audience, excited in the highest degree by the impassioned words which had fallen from his lips, flocked around him, eager to be ranked among his followers. Old men were seen bringing forward their children, wives their husbands, and widowed mothers their sons, sending them under his paternal care to fight the battles of their country. It must have been a noble sight, and the cause thus supported could not fail.

Nearly three hundred men of the frontier churches that day enlisted under his banner; and the gown then thrown off was worn for the last time. Henceforth his footsteps were destined for a new career.[29]

Please note that the above accounting of the occasion begins with "a well-authenticated anecdote is told of him". This is not some cleverly contrived story to make the family name of Muhlenberg famous. Peter Muhlenberg and his brother, Frederick, both served in the efforts of the American Revolution and had significant contributions in the newly formed government without made-up stories. In fact, the biography begins with the following Preface:

In submitting the following pages to the public, the author may be permitted to hope that his trifling contribution to the Revolutionary history of the country will not be received with disfavour. A belief that the materials were of some value, was the first inducement to publication. The second, was to place the services of General Muhlenberg in their proper light; in doing which, however, he has constantly endeavoured to avoid being

---

[29] Muhlenberg, Henry Augustus, *The Life of Major-General Peter Muhlenberg of the Revolutionary Army*, (Philadelphia: Cary and Hart; C. Sherman, printer, 1849), 52-53

biassed by the natural prejudice in favour of a relative. The work itself will show that he has anxiously consulted all accessible authorities, and at least endeavoured to draw from them impartial conclusions.[30]

What this historic event projects very clearly is that the members of the Black Robe Regiment were intensively dedicated to the need for the overthrow of tyranny in the protection of religious freedom. In particular, Pastor Muhlenberg is a fantastic example of the fire that should burn in the heart of the American Christian who yearns to maintain the freedoms we have been so graciously afforded by Almighty God.

Another such man was Reverend Jonas Clarke. Many are not familiar with his name, but American Christians certainly should be. The destination of Paul Revere on the fateful night of April 18, 1775 was ultimately Reverend Clarke's home. The pastor was housing two very special patriots that evening: Samuel Adams and John Hancock. Both of these men were quite prominent in the scheme of the resistance, and two of the most wanted by the British.

Pastor Clarke was also very well known to be in support of the colonial cause in pushing back against the tyranny of the English Monarch. His sermons were of the typical Black Robe Regiment sort.

---

[30] Muhlenberg, Henry Augustus, *The Life of Major-General Peter Muhlenberg of the Revolutionary Army*, (Philadelphia: Cary and Hart; C. Sherman, printer, 1849), p.5

Once a simple farmer and preacher, "...when the trouble between the Colonies and the mother country commenced, he stepped at once from his obscurity, and became known throughout all the region as one of the most uncompromising patriots of the day. Earnestly, yet without passion, he discussed from the pulpit the great questions at issue, and that powerful voice thundered forth the principles of personal, civil, and religious liberty, and the right of resistance, in tones as earnest and effective as it had the doctrine of salvation by the cross."[31]

In the early hours of April 19, 1775 Reverend Clarke was asked by the men staying in his home if the men of Lexington would be ready if it came to a fight. Reverend Clarke is famous to have said, "I have trained them for this very hour."[32] One year later, as the anniversary of the event drew near, Pastor Clarke delivered a sermon recollecting what had occurred in the early hours of that April morning. He was more determined than ever to press his congregation toward defending their rights to being free.

Once the British surged past Lexington, they encountered another group in Concord which were also led by their pastor. Reverend William Emerson, pastor of First Perish in Concord, Massachusetts, had called his congregation of men together as well. He had prepared them for the moment when they would need to fight to defend their families and freedom for "Behold

---

[31] Headley, J. T., *The Chaplains and Clergy of the Revolution* (New York: Charles Scribner, 1864) 75

[32] Cole, Franklin P., ed. *They Preached Liberty* (Indianapolis: Liberty Press) 39

God himself is with us for our Captain and his priests with sounding trumpets to cry alarm..."[33]

One month later would come the day the "Regulars", as the British soldiers were commonly known, would march into their community. When the alarm rang to gather the forces together, Emerson grabbed his musket and in his robe headed to the center of town. It was there that the older men of the community gathered to discuss their circumstances. It was at that point that Reverend Emerson stated, "Let us stand our ground. If we die, let us die here!"[34] Not long thereafter the red coats could be seen across the horizon as the morning sun glistened off their rifles against the clear blue sky.

The pastor began to move among the troops encouraging them in what was about to take place. Coming across one young man, Harry Gould, who was obviously rattled by the severity of the moment, Pastor Emerson proclaimed, "Stand your ground Harry! Your cause is just and God will bless you."[35]

When the dust had settled and the Regulars were forced back toward Boston, the battle for American independence had begun. While it is true that no formal declaration had been made for separation from England, the die was cast for the hot iron of war to be poured into it.

---

[33] French, Allen, *The Day of Concord and Lexington: The Nineteenth of April, 1775* (Boston: Little, Brown and Company, 1925) 150

[34] Hackett Fisher, David, *Paul Revere's Ride* (New York: Oxford University Press, 1994) 204

[35] Ibid, 205

With all of the intensive display of support from Colonial pulpits the governmental agents assigned to New England were unsettled at the very least. Reports were sent back across the ocean to the monarch citing extreme unrest. It is commonly reported that one such British governor became so frustrated that he is known to report to the King, "If you ask an American who is his master, he'll tell you he has none. And he has no governor but Jesus Christ."[36]

"In his article *The Forgotten Holiday,* Tom Barrett states, "I do not consider it a stretch at all to say that were it not for the pastors and churches of colonial America, our land would be a British colony today."[37] It is apparent that the pastorate of the mid to late 18th Century held much sway on the culture's view of the way England's new laws and movements toward stronger control of the colonies were viewed.

The Black Robe Regiment resounded in a collective voice which echoed throughout the colonies with the call to freedom from oppression. These tones reverberated through the souls of the various government bodies comprised of representatives from communities everywhere. While there are, admittedly, voices pressing for freedom that did not follow a Christian drumbeat, the overwhelming number most assuredly did so.

---

[36] Niles, Hezekiah, *Principals and Acts of the Revolution in America* (Baltimore: William Ogden Niles, 1822) 418

[37] Examiner.com, The *Black Regiment – The Bane of the British – The Soul of the American Republic.* Last modified January 9, 2012, http://www.examiner.com/article/the-black-regiment-the-bane-of-the-british-the-soul-of-the-american-republic [accessed July 16, 2013]

It is evident that most of those famously engaged in the elements of designing the United States of America in its government were Christian of one form or another. Many have attempted to label the majority of those, and especially those whose names are recognizable by the common citizen, as deists.

In order to conduct a reasonable discussion on this matter, the dictionary is to be consulted. What is *deism*? Deism is a "belief in the existence of a God on the evidence of reason and nature only, with rejection of supernatural revelation", and a "belief in a God who created the world but has since remained indifferent to it."[38]

So, a deist is one who believes that God exists, set the world in motion, but has no interaction into its activity. He set it up like a terrarium and now simply observes its occupants. This is a God who would not interfere in the actions of anyone or anything which exists in His creation.

The following motion was made by Benjamin Franklin to the Constitutional Convention on June 28, 1787:

> In this situation of this Assembly, groping as it were in the dark to find political truth, and scarce able to distinguish it when presented to us, how has it happened, Sir, that we have not hitherto once thought of humbly applying to the Father of lights to illuminate our understandings? In the beginning of the Contest with Great Britain, when

---

[38] deism. Dictionary.com. *Dictionary.com Unabridged*. Random House, Inc. http://dictionary.reference.com/browse/deism (accessed: July 24, 2013).

we were sensible of danger we had daily prayer in this room for the divine protection.- **Our prayers, Sir, were heard, and they were graciously answered. All of us who were engaged in the struggle must have observed frequent instances of a superintending providence in our favor.**

To that kind providence we owe this happy opportunity of consulting in peace on the means of establishing our future national felicity. **And have we now forgotten that powerful friend? or do we imagine that we no longer need his assistance? I have lived, Sir, a long time, and the longer I live, the more convincing proofs I see of this truth- that God Governs in the affairs of men. And if a sparrow cannot fall to the ground without his notice, is it probable that an empire can rise without his aid? We have been assured, Sir, in the sacred writings, that "except the Lord build the House they labour in vain that build it." I firmly believe this; and I also believe that without his concurring aid we shall succeed in this political building no better, than the Builders of Babel**: We shall be divided by our little partial local interests; our projects will be confounded, and we ourselves shall become a reproach and bye word down to future ages. And what is worse, mankind may hereafter from this unfortunate instance, despair of establishing Governments by Human wisdom and leave it to chance, war and conquest.

I therefore beg leave to move-that **henceforth prayers imploring the assistance of Heaven, and its blessings**

on our deliberations, be held in this Assembly every morning before we proceed to business, and that one or more of the Clergy of this City be requested to officiate in that Service-[39]

In addition to this highly noted proposal by Dr. Franklin, he included a theological creed in his autobiography which clearly stated:

[I believe] That there is one God, who made all things.

That he governs the world by his providence.

That he ought to be worshiped by adoration, prayer, and thanksgiving.

But that the most acceptable service of God is doing good to man.

That the soul is immortal.

And that God will certainly reward virtue and punish vice, either here or hereafter.[40]

What becomes very clear upon proper examination of the facts is that Benjamin Franklin was *not* a deist, believing, by his own

---

[39] *Journals of the Continental Congress, 1774-1789,* ed. Worthington C. Ford et al. (Washington, D.C., 1904-37), 450-452 Bolded print by author for emphasis

[40] Franklin, Benjamin, *The Autobiography of Benjamin Franklin,* ed. Charles W. Eliot L.L.D. (New York, P. F. Collier & Son Company, 1909)

account, that God "governs the world by his providence".[41] It also is apparent that, according to the motion presented before the Constitutional Convention, prayer was offered up "daily" during the Continental Congress proceedings of the Revolutionary War.

Due to the varying faiths of the founders there was a stir created when prayer was suggested to begin each session. Because of their varied approaches to religion the founding fathers in the early days of the gathering could not agree upon a prayer to be said, or who should lead in such prayer. John Adams noted in a letter to his wife Abigail, "we were so divided in religious sentiments; some Episcopalians, some Quakers, some Anabaptists, some Presbyterians, and some Congregationalists, that we could not join in the same act of worship."[42] Samuel Adams rose to the occasion and suggested Reverend Jacob Duche' could be agreed upon by all due to the fact that he was a "man of piety and virtue, who was at the same time a friend to his country".[43] The motion presented by Samuel Adams was passed, and the Reverend Duche' approached about offering the time of devotion the next morning.

The Reverend arrived the next morning, offered some of the standard prayers of the day, and read from the established "collect", as Adams referred to it. The Bible reading for that

---

[41] Franklin, Benjamin, *The Autobiography of Benjamin Franklin,* ed. Charles W. Eliot L.L.D. (New York, P. F. Collier & Son Company, 1909)

[42] Adams, John. Letter from John Adams to Abigail Adams, 16 September 1774. 4 pages. Original manuscript from the Adams Family Papers, Massachusetts Historical Society.

[43] Ibid

Morning was Psalm 35. The following is excerpts from that Psalm:

> [1] Plead my cause, O Lord, with them that strive with me: fight against them that fight against me.

> [2] Take hold of shield and buckler, and stand up for mine help.

> [3] Draw out also the spear, and stop the way against them that persecute me: say unto my soul, I am thy salvation.

> [7] For without cause have they hid for me their net in a pit, which without cause they have digged for my soul.

> [8] Let destruction come upon him at unawares; and let his net that he hath hid catch himself: into that very destruction let him fall.

> [14] I behaved myself as though he had been my friend or brother: I bowed down heavily, as one that mourneth for his mother.

> [15] But in mine adversity they rejoiced, and gathered themselves together: yea, the abjects gathered themselves together against me, and I knew it not; they did tear me, and ceased not:

> [16] With hypocritical mockers in feasts, they gnashed upon me with their teeth.

[17] Lord, how long wilt thou look on? rescue my soul from their destructions, my darling from the lions.

[28] And my tongue shall speak of thy righteousness and of thy praise all the day long.[44]

At the conclusion of the reading, the Reverend fell to his knees and cried out in a prayer of his own making. The prayer he delivered thundered the desperate cry which was being felt throughout the colonies.

...look down in mercy, we beseech Thee, on these our American States, who have fled to Thee from the rod of the oppressor and thrown themselves on Thy gracious protection, desiring to be henceforth dependent only on Thee. To Thee have they appealed for the righteousness of their cause; to Thee do they now look up for that countenance and support, which Thou alone canst give. Take them, therefore, Heavenly Father, under Thy nurturing care; give them wisdom in Council and valor in the field; defeat the malicious designs of our cruel adversaries; convince them of the unrighteousness of their Cause and if they persist in their sanguinary purposes, of own unerring justice, sounding in their hearts, constrain them to drop the weapons of war from their unnerved hands in the day of battle!

Be Thou present, O God of wisdom, and direct the councils of this honorable assembly; enable them to

---

[44]   Psalm 35 (King James Version)

settle things on the best and surest foundation. That the scene of blood may be speedily closed; that order, harmony and peace may be effectually restored, and truth and justice, religion and piety, prevail and flourish amongst the people.[45]

This Bible passage and the ensuing prayer, as John Adams recounts it, "filled the bosom of every man present".[46] It was this type of prayer, as resounded through the room at Carpenter's Hall on September 7, 1774, which Benjamin Franklin was referring to as he addressed the Constitutional Convention some thirteen years later.

Each day which passed in those early months of the Revolution brought with it greater restrictions and more impassioned determination from the Throne of England to bring the "rabble" under control. More and more the claxons sounding the alarm against tyranny clamored for the attention of the colonists. No one was untouched as the sides squared off. It was a true David and Goliath story. The greatest army and navy on the planet were launching an assault against their own. The colonials were a ragtag group of dwellers on their own soil from varied walks of life assembled to lay claim once and for all on the ability to live in a free nation.

---

[45] Office of the Chaplain, United States House of Representatives, First Prayer of the Continental Congress, 1774, September 7, 1774, http://chaplain.house.gov/archive/continental.html

[46] Adams, John. Letter from John Adams to Abigail Adams, 16 September 1774. 4 pages. Original manuscript from the Adams Family Papers, Massachusetts Historical Society.

Only four and a half short years had passed since a British force had fired on a "mob" assembled in Boston. John Adams had led the defense for the soldiers and had won. Now he sat in the chambers of the group organizing a rebellion. Earlier in the year of 1774, England had brought resolutions against the town of Boston, shutting down its port. Another of these "Intolerable Acts" was the suspension of trial by jury due to an enactment of a system of martial law. And, further, the King enacted a Quartering Act, requiring each household in America under English rule to provide for living quarters and sustenance for the British forces. Each of these, and others, mounted into a groundswell of resistance from the populace.

The Continental Congress gathered in secret in Philadelphia to attempt to formulate a response to these violations of their rights. Those supporting the Crown, or Tories, as they were known, muttered in anger against the proceedings. Ultimately, however, the inevitable raced toward the group as recognizable as the thundering of thousands of war horses pressing into battle.

Each offer proffered to King George III and the members of Parliament was met with increased attempts to tighten the Motherland's grip around the throat of the citizenry of New England. When a notice was returned to England demanding the rights of Englishmen, it angered the Monarch. With the pulpits of America defending the rights of free men, and the continued lack of amicable response from across the ocean, the representatives of a free society were hard pressed to inch ever closer to independence.

CHAMBER OF THE CONTINENTIAL CONGRESS
Independence Hall
Philadelphia, Pennsylvania

Endowed by Our Creator

In CONGRESS, July 4, 1776
The unanimous Declaration of the
thirteen united States of America

When in the Course of human events it becomes necessary for one people to dissolve the political bands which have connected them with another and to assume among the powers of the earth, the separate and equal station to which the Laws of Nature and of Nature's God entitle them, a decent respect to the opinions of mankind requires that they should declare the causes which impel them to the separation.

We hold these truths to be self-evident, that all men are created equal, that they are endowed by their Creator with certain unalienable Rights, that among these are Life, Liberty and the pursuit of Happiness. — That to secure these rights, Governments are instituted among Men, deriving their just powers from the consent of the governed...

With these words begins one of the most recognized documents in world history, The Declaration of Independence of the United States of America, July 4, 1776. Laid out in this document are the reasons the colonies were declaring themselves independent of rule by England. The violations included were those which went against the principles and values they had been taught. These ideals were thundered from the pulpits of the Christian churches throughout the land, and had been heard by the majority of those assembled to conduct this business of freedom.

Foundational to the grievances submitted to the king and parliament was the fact that the very edicts of God Himself had been dishonored. They were taking upon themselves the position that the "Laws of Nature and of Nature's God entitle(d) them." These were a people "endowed by their Creator with certain unalienable Rights". Some of those rights, "Life, Liberty and the pursuit of Happiness."

God was at the epicenter of the rumblings which formed the United States of America. A Creator granted these rights. It was not a cataclysmic explosion of stuff hurled into space and settled into balls of molten goo which eventually somehow *miraculously* of its own accord effected change in a changeless environment. No Creator... no Rights.

And to secure these rights, Governments are instituted "among Men". These crafters of one of the greatest documents ever to outline the case for freedom knew where the power to be free came from. Jesus spoke of this freedom in John 8:34-36. "... Verily, verily, I say unto you, Whosoever committeth sin is the servant of sin. And the servant abideth not in the house for ever: but the Son abideth ever. If the Son therefore shall make you free, ye shall be free indeed."

While the names of Thomas Jefferson, John Adams, Benjamin Franklin, Samuel Adams and John Hancock are prominent among the signers of the Declaration of Independence, there are fifty-one others who committed themselves to the task of independence. Were these men committed to personal freedom driven by a purpose devoid of godly influence? Absolutely not!

As mentioned previously, a revival was sweeping across the countryside in New England. Messages ranged from the calm, to the sublime, and onward to the fiery. Each sermon explained the biblical support and reasoning for moving away from a governing body that was increasingly becoming oppressive. And these were being heard by those in positions of legislative influence.

The years preceding the "unanimous Declaration of Independence" were tumultuous times of repressive actions by a monarchy bent on punishment, nearing indentured servitude. The majority of the families comprising the colonies were settled in the land through ancestors seeking a life free from the bondage of religious persecution. It is documented that these craftsmen of the American experience were of a nature molded in the heat of conflict between the godly freedom to exercise their faith and the iron-fisted assault on their livelihoods, including religious freedom.

Each man who spent untold hours in that enclosed meeting hall in Philadelphia during the Continental Congress sessions carried with him the solemn duty to represent his colony in defending the rights of freemen. He also held the most unenviable position of standing in opposition to the Crown, and all the forces represented thereby.

The individual members of that gathering came from the reaches of the far north to the southernmost point of New England. In each of these colonies varying bodies of representation had been placed to allow for them to speak on behalf of those from all facets of life on the subjects brought before the group. Almost all of the men had served as a member of their respective legislatures in the colony from which they hailed. All were committed to the cause.

What is not commonly understood is the reasons which built the need for the Declaration of Independence. Tremendous shifts in world power had recently taken place, and England held overwhelming power in America. In order to secure the hold on what was increasingly viewed as a people who had become a bit too autonomous, the Crown began to inject its influence into New England.

England, in 1763 had signed the *Treaty of Paris,* ending the war in which it had defeated both the French and Spanish. By doing so it gained all lands east of the Mississippi River in the present day United States of America, several Caribbean islands, and Canada. With the war against France and Spain over, England was able to shift its focus toward American conquest once again.

To launch their purposes several *Acts* were placed into law beginning in 1765. The people of New England had become accustomed to the focus of the monarchy being elsewhere, and these new restrictive laws were met with intensive disfavor. Protests were launched by those across the land who opposed such measures. The fires of revolution were beginning to be fanned.

Much has already been said about the ministers throughout New England and their support of a movement toward independence. Leaders arose from those congregations who now served in houses of representation in each territory. Spurred on by their distaste for the British government's increasing grip, and the biblical support being delivered in houses of worship, many began to call for a final solution: complete independence from England.

While only fifty-six members were able to sign the Declaration, many more had helped frame the events from which this unprecedented document was formulated. One such member of the revolution is Patrick Henry. On May 29, 1765 he proposed a resolution restricting the ability of the English government to enact taxation on the Virginia Colony.

Resolved, therefor that the General Assembly of this Colony have the only and exclusive Right and Power to lay Taxes and Impositions upon the inhabitants of this Colony and that every Attempt to vest such Power in any person or persons whatsoever other than the General Assembly aforesaid has a manifest Tendency to destroy British as well as American Freedom.[47]

This resolution, in addition to four others similarly presented, offered the rights of Virginians to be taxed only by proper representation. They also laid out what would ultimately be the principles by which the Declaration of Independence would be fashioned. In support of his resolution, he stood and delivered the first of the lively oratories for which he would ultimately become famous. The exact text of the speech appears to be lost in history, but a recounting of it indicates the fire which burned within him as he spoke.

It was in the midst of this magnificent debate, while he was descanting on the tyranny of the obnoxious Act, that he exclaimed, in a voice of thunder, and with the look of a god, "Caesar had his Brutus - Charles the first, his Cromwell - and George the third —" ('Treason,' cried the Speaker - 'treason, treason,' echoed from every part of the House. - It was one of those trying moments which is decisive of character.) - Henry faltered not an instant; but rising to a loftier attitude, and fixing on the Speaker an eye of the most determined fire, he finished his sentence

---

[47] UShistory.org: *Created and Hosted by the Independence Hall Association in Philadelphia,* http://www.ushistory.org/declaration/related/vsa65.htm (accessed July 25, 2013)

with the firmest emphasis) "may profit by their example. If this be treason, make the most of it."[48]

Henry's proposition was passed by the House of Burgesses that day, and quickly recanted the next. But not before the news of the speech given by the young twenty-nine year old had gained him a reputation throughout Virginia and on to all of New England.

Ten years later, on March 23, 1775, in the same legislature he delivered what has come to be one of the clarion calls as for independence. It is this speech for which he is most well known.

No man thinks more highly than I do of the patriotism, as well as abilities, of the very worthy gentlemen who have just addressed the House. But different men often see the same subject in different lights; and, therefore, I hope that it will not be thought disrespectful to those gentlemen, if, entertaining as I do opinions of a character very opposite to theirs, I shall speak forth my sentiments freely and without reserve.

This is no time for ceremony. The question before the House is one of awful moment to this country. For my own part I consider it as nothing less than a question of freedom or slavery; and in proportion to the magnitude of the subject ought to be the freedom of the debate.

---

[48] Wirt, William, *Sketches of the Life and Character of Patrick Henry* (Philadelphia: James Webster, 1817)

It is only in this way that we can hope to arrive at truth, and fulfill the great responsibility which we hold to God and our country. Should I keep back my opinions at such a time, through fear of giving offense, I should consider myself as guilty of treason towards my country, and of an act of disloyalty towards the majesty of heaven, which I revere above all earthly kings.

*   *   *

If we wish to be free—if we mean to preserve inviolate those inestimable privileges for which we have been so long contending—if we mean not basely to abandon the noble struggle in which we have been so long engaged, and which we have pledged ourselves never to abandon until the glorious object of our contest shall be obtained, we must fight! I repeat it, sir, we must fight! **An appeal to arms and to the God of Hosts is all that is left us!**

*   *   *

Sir, we are not weak, if we make a proper use of the means which the God of nature hath placed in our power. Three millions of people, armed in the holy cause of liberty, and in such a country as that which we possess, are invincible by any force which our enemy can send against us. Besides, sir, we shall not fight our battles alone. **There is a just God who presides over the destinies of nations, and who will raise up friends to fight our battles for us.**

The battle, sir, is not to the strong alone; it is to the vigilant, the active, the brave. Besides, sir, we have no election. If we were base enough to desire it, it is now too late to retire from the contest. There is no retreat but in submission and slavery! Our chains are forged! Their clanking may be heard on the plains of Boston! The war is inevitable—and let it come! I repeat it, sir, let it come!

It is in vain, sir, to extenuate the matter. Gentlemen may cry, "Peace! Peace!"—but there is no peace. The war is actually begun! The next gale that sweeps from the north will bring to our ears the clash of resounding arms! Our brethren are already in the field! Why stand we here idle? What is it that gentlemen wish? What would they have? Is life so dear, or peace so sweet, as to be purchased at the price of chains and slavery? Forbid it, Almighty God! I know not what course others may take; but as for me, give me liberty, or give me death![49]

With these words the patriot recited words which were unformed in the mouths of some within the colonies, but most assuredly beat within their hearts. It was with true conviction that he stated clearly that this battle was not theirs alone, but would be fought by the Almighty God of heaven. And it was this type of conviction which drove the patriots standing for the freedom which was given them through that one true God.

---

[49] Lit2Go, Historic American Documents by FCIT http://etc.usf.edu/lit2go/133/historic-american-documents/4956/patrick-henrys-speech-to-the-virginia-house-of-burgess-richmond-virginia-march-23-1775/ (accessed July 25, 2013) Bolded print by author for emphasis

The Continental Congress had convened over the course of the two years preceding their climactic week beginning Monday, July 1, 1776. Many "olive branches" had been extended to King George III asking for respite from the imposed laws which were restricting their freedom and causing great economic and social crisis throughout New England. Each attempt was met by rejection and further impositions.

After considerable debate, and with a retreat by the Tory factions from the chambers, the Continental Congress passed a resolution to draft a declaration of their intentions to separate from the motherland. John Adams described his perception of the future of American to Abigail, his wife.

> It is the Will of Heaven, that the two Countries should be sundered forever. It may be the Will of Heaven that America shall suffer Calamities still more wasting and Distresses yet more dreadful. If this is to be the Case, it will have this good Effect, at least: it will inspire Us with many Virtues, which We have not, and correct many Errors, Follies, and Vices, which threaten to disturb, dishonor, and destroy Us.

*　*　*

> The Second Day of July 1776, will be the most memorable Epocha, in the History of America.-I am apt to believe that it will be celebrated, by succeeding Generation, as the great anniversary Festival. It ought to be commemorated, as the Day of Deliverance by solemn Acts of Devotion to God Almighty. It ought to solemnized

with Pomp and Parade, with Shews, Games, Sports, Guns, Bells, Bonfires and Illuminations from one End of this Continent to the other from this Time forward forever more.[50]

John Adams realized the power which brought independence to America. He recognized that there was no other which could have brought them to this point in history. His suggestion that celebrations should include "solemn Acts of Devotion to God Almighty" emphasizes his personal assurance that it was an orchestration by God Himself that America be free.

The Declaration of Independence provides insight into the religious undertones of the American Revolution. The opening paragraph, presented at the beginning of this chapter, specifically outlines that the declaration has been undertaken to explain the reasoning of such document, which is required upon such an event. They were intent to "assume among the powers of the earth, the separate and equal station to which the Laws of Nature and of Nature's God entitle them" And "among these" rights were those of "Life, Liberty and the pursuit of Happiness".

They were entitled to be independent of the oppressive government of England, not by a feeling of pains involved in their lives, but by the very "Laws of Nature and Nature's God". It was a divine appointment under the guidance of heavenly Providence.

---

[50]   Adams, John. Letter from John Adams to Abigail Adams, 3 July 1776. 3 pages. Original manuscript from the Adams Family Papers, Massachusetts Historical Society.

The first, most sacred, of reasons presented to King George III must have raised the monarch's ire. This rabble which had left the shores of England over the previous two centuries to settle where they may practice unauthorized practices in worship, were instructing him in the ways of God. They are "created equal" and are "endowed by their Creator with certain unalienable rights". These were not rights contrived of manmade ideals, but are inarguable rights granted by Almighty God. In this they were stating that not even the King could question them in this.

With that these representatives of the oppressed continued by setting out the violations of these 'inalienable' rights. The King had refused them the rights of countrymen in representation. He had violated the sacred trust of protecting them by attacking them himself, inappropriately quartering troops among them, and singling them out for taxation without having a voice in the matter. These, among other similar reasons set forth, are outlined in this document.

After settling the logic behind their separation, they acknowledged the known consequences. In doing so, they once again reiterated their trust in being able to carry out the action they were putting their hand and heart to.

We, therefore, the Representatives of the united States of America, in General Congress, Assembled, appealing to the Supreme Judge of the world for rectitude of our intentions, do, in the Name, and by the Authority of the good People of these Colonies, solemnly publish and declare, That these United Colonies are, and of a Right ought to be Free and Independent States; that they are Absolved from all Allegiance to the British Crown, and that all political connection between them and the State of Great Britain, is and ought to be totally dissolved; and that as Free and Independent States, they have full Power to levy War, conclude Peace, contract Alliances, establish Commerce, and to do all other Acts and Things which Independent States may of right do.

In appealing to the "Supreme Judge of the world" for the righteous reasoning (rectitude) of their intentions, they once again asserted that their cause was a just one, viable through His truth. Essentially they were saying that they were pronouncing themselves independent of Great Britain under God's authority.

Finally, they would stake the entire declaration on the ultimate elements of equity afforded them.

> ...for the support of this Declaration, with a firm reliance on the protection of divine Providence, we mutually pledge to each other our Lives, our Fortunes and our sacred Honor.

This was not a petty undertaking. By signing this document each of the men present were placing their family, the entirety of their worldly goods, and their very reputations as collateral. The intentions of the King were clear in such matters. Orders had already been given for the arrest of Samuel Adams and John Hancock that they might be hanged for treason. In placing their signature alongside these men, each one had brought upon themselves the same fate.

It is for this reason that they placed their trust in a "firm reliance on the protection of divine Providence". Only God would help this fledgling nation stand in the face of the greatest military force on the planet. Only God could guide the revolutionaries in their quest for freedom. For it was quite clear that only God had the capability to bring down Goliath.

George Washington had been given the command of the Continental Army by an act of the Congress on June 15, 1775, raising him in status from a colonel to a general. His experience in the French and Indian War from prior years gave him an advantage over others who desired such a post. Ironically, General Washington did not request the assignment, but it was pressed upon him by those within the Continental Congress of which he was part. In a letter to his wife, June 18, 1775, Washington informed her of the appointment.

> ...It has been determined in Congress, that the whole Army raised for the defence of the American Cause shall be put under my care, and that it is necessary for me to proceed immediately to Boston to take upon me the Command of it. You may believe me my dear Patcy, when I assure you, in the most solemn manner, that, so far from seeking this appointment I have used every endeavour in my power to avoid it, not only from my unwillingness to part with you and the Family, but from a consciousness of its being a trust too great for my Capacity and that I should enjoy more real happiness and felicity in one month with you, at home, than I have the most distant prospect of reaping abroad... I shall rely therefore, confidently, on that Providence which

has heretofore preserved & been bountiful to me, not doubting but that I shall return safe to you in the fall... [51]

General, ultimately President, Washington was known as a man of faith. There are those disputing the validity of the prayer in the woods which allegedly took place just before the battle at Valley Forge. While we may not know that the prayer took place in the setting portrayed in the paintings we see, one may certainly justify the fact that prayer most definitely took place. Washington was a man devoted to prayer. He kept a prayer journal. One of the most fascinating prayers offered in the journal reads as follows:

O eternal and everlasting God, I presume to present myself this morning before thy Divine majesty, beseeching thee to accept of my humble and hearty thanks, that it hath pleased thy great goodness to keep and preserve me the night past from all the dangers poor mortals are subject to, and has given me sweet and pleasant sleep, whereby I find my body refreshed and comforted for performing the duties of this day, in which I beseech thee to defend me from all perils of body and soul. Direct my thoughts, words and work, wash away my sins in the immaculate blood of the lamb, and purge my heart by thy holy spirit, from the dross of my natural corruption, that I may with more freedom of mind and liberty of will serve thee, the ever lasting God, in righteousness and

---

[51] Washington, George, Letter from George Washington to Martha Washington, 18 June 1775, in Martha Washington Item #87 http://www.marthawashington.us/items/show/87 (accessed July 25, 2013)

holiness this day, and all the days of my life. Increase my faith in the sweet promises of the gospel; give me repentance from dead works; pardon my wanderings, & direct my thoughts unto thyself, the God of my salvation; teach me how to live in thy fear, labor in thy service, and ever to run in the ways of thy commandments; make me always watchful over my heart, that neither the terrors of conscience, the loathing of holy duties, the love of sin, nor an unwillingness to depart this life, may cast me into a spiritual slumber, but daily frame me more 7 more into the likeness of thy son Jesus Christ, that living in thy fear, and dying in thy favor, I may in thy appointed time attain the resurrection of the just unto eternal life bless my family, friends & kindred unite us all in praising & glorifying thee in all our works begun, continued, and ended, when we shall come to make our last account before thee blessed saviour, who hath taught us thus to pray, our Father, & c. [52]

What a glorious prayer! Thanking God for the restful night's sleep, asking for blessing into the coming day, and asking repentance for his innate sin, and more, all wrapped into what is obviously one of the most sincere prayers delivered. Could this man have been a deist? Absolutely not!

In his direction of the troops, General Washington delivered the following General Orders, casting all doubt aside that he was Christian by nature:

---

[52] Johnstone, William Jackson, *George Washington, the Christian* (New York: The Abingdon Press 1919), 24-35

The Honorable Continental Congress having been pleased to allow a Chaplain to each Regiment,… The Colonels or commanding officers of each regiment are directed to procure Chaplains accordingly; persons of good Characters and exemplary lives-To see that all inferior officers and soldiers pay them a suitable respect and attend carefully upon religious exercises: The blessing and protection of Heaven are at all times necessary but especially so in times of public distress and danger-The General hopes and trusts, that every officer, and man, will endeavour so to live, and act, as becomes a Christian Soldier defending the dearest Rights and Liberties of his country.[53]

It is apparent that when the General was speaking of chaplains, he was speaking of those of the Christian faith, since each military person was to conduct themselves "as becomes a Christian Soldier". Many other writings of George Washington in his service in the military and in elected public service will be shared in this writing. Suffice it to say that the General gave much glory to God and His sustaining power.

The War for Independence raged against great odds. It was a long and arduous conflict. The early defeats tore at the new nation's resolve. But they had placed their "firm reliance upon the protection of divine Providence". And it was God that gave the victory!

---

[53] Washington, George, *The Papers of George Washington: Revolutionary War Series,* Philander D. Chase, ed. (Charlottesville: University Press of Virginia, 1988) 245-247

The Body of
B. Franklin. Printer.
Like the Cover of an old Book.
Its Contents torn out.
And Stript of its Lettering & Gilding.
Lies here. Food for Worms.
But the Work shall not be lost.
For it will as he believ'd
appear once more,
In a new and more elegant Edition
Corrected and improved
By the Author.

———

(This epitaph written by Franklin as a young
man, was not intended to be used. His nearby
gravestone was prepared in exact accordance
with the instructions contained in his will.)

———

This gravesite restored
by the Poor Richard Club
of Philadelphia
through the generosity
of Howard C. Story
in memory of his parents
Edward A. and Mary Elizabeth Story

PLACARD NEAR BENJAMIN FRANKLIN'S GRAVE
Christ Church
Philadelphia, Pennsylvania

Foundations of Freedom

So much has been said in recent years about the 'fact' that America has been established on the basis of religious neutrality. The truth is that our United States have a deeply religious heritage based on Judeo-Christian principles which date back two thousand years and more. The principles which governed those who stepped foot on this land, have been Christian since Columbus and forward, as noted previously.

The great ones who fought for our freedom to live apart from England were no different. They had a desire to worship God freely, in whichever manner they chose. The earliest letters penned by the men, and women, who resisted the monarchy across the ocean in every way of documents, military service, and maintaining the home front spoke highly of the God of heaven.

Yes, there were those parties contrary to the faith, as there always have been. Thomas Paine is lifted up by those set in proving America is atheistic in its origin as one of those questioning faith in several of his writings. What is not readily known is that, while he resisted the practice of faith as a direct influence to government action, this was probably due to his strong fear that a national church would rise as that in England.

Mister Paine is primarily known for his production of the pamphlet entitled *Common Sense*, a writing which helped fan the flames of the fight for freedom. General George Washington had select portions of this pamphlet read to the troops at Valley Forge before their campaign began in crossing the Delaware. In it the revolutionary author intoned:

> The cause of America is in a great measure the cause of all mankind.[54]

> *   *   *

> But where says some is the King of America? I'll tell you Friend, he reigns above, and doth not make havoc of mankind like the Royal Brute of Britain.[55]

> *   *   *

> Yet that we may not appear to be defective even in earthly honors, let a day be solemnly set apart for

---

[54]   Paine, Thomas, *Common Sense*, (Philadelphia: R. Bell, 1776) Introduction
[55]   Ibid, Thoughts on the Present State of American Affairs

proclaiming the charter; let it be placed on the divine law, the Word of God; let a crown be placed thereon.[56]

*　　*　　*

The Almighty implanted in us these unextinguishable feelings for good and wise purposes. They are the guardians of His image in our heart. They distinguished us from the herd of common animals.[57]

The pamphlet is founded upon biblical principles which Paine used to instruct the populace in New England that there should, in fact, be no king. The Bible's chronicling of the Israelites request for a king at various points in their history is the foundation for the patriot's insistence that no king should be set over a people, and that, instead, God should reign in man's freedom.

Amazingly, nearly twenty years later Thomas Paine would write a book released in three parts, the first two in 1794 and 1795, and the third part twelve years later in 1807 in response to challenges by a Bishop. In 1776 he lauded the Bible's wise instruction that there be no king save God Himself. In these releases he attacks the very Word of God he founded his first work on.

He begins the work by stating that he wanted to write these works "for several years past". He then proceeds, through the

---

[56] Paine, Thomas, *Common Sense*, (Philadelphia: R. Bell, 1776) Thoughts on the Present State of American Affairs

[57] Ibid

first two parts, to explain away any organized religion by any group: namely the Jews, the Christians, and those following Mohammed. He begins his work by setting up his reasoning for developing the writing, and then he sets forth his "profession of faith":

> I believe in one God, and no more; and I hope for happiness beyond this life.[58]

Thomas Paine is the one Founding Father which states very clearly in his later writing while in France that he is a Deist. He believes that God may be found in the science of creation, and that the one true God is Creator, without denial. If one reads his *Age of Reason*, you hear the words of one attempting to be intellectual and grasping at what he sees as absurdity in Scripture. His 'reasoning' for this is that no one group surely has the absolute answer.

John Adams, strong proponent of the Declaration of Independence, first Vice President and second President of the United States of America, responded to Paine's assault on Christianity by saying, "The Christian religion is, above all the Religions that ever prevailed or existed in ancient or modern times, the religion of Wisdom, Virtue, Equity, and Humanity. Let the Blackguard Paine say what he will; it is Resignation to God, it is Goodness itself to Man."[59]

---

[58] Paine, Thomas, *The Age of Reason: Being an Investigation into True and Fabulous Theology*, (Paris: Barrois, 1794) Part I

[59] Butterfield, L. H., ed. *The Diary and Autobiography of John Adams*, (Cambridge, MA: The Belknap Press of Harvard University Press, 1962), Vol. 3, 233-234 quoted in William J. Federer, ed., *America's God*

Some of Paine's strongest arguments against the Bible and its truths of God was that the Church had imposed such beliefs as purgatory, indulgences which could be bought, and other extra-faith practices. He also focused on there being many translations of the Bible throughout time, and that no written record of the first order could be found. Because he could not touch them, he dismissed them and did not believe in them. In this same manner, I contend that I have only heard of Thomas Paine in writings accredited to himself and others. Yet I did not see him pen the works. I have seen paintings of his supposed likeness, but I never met him personally, and therefore, I do not believe in him or his writings. Therefore, Thomas Paine did not exist. This is the absurdity in which he *reasons* away the Bible as God's Word.

Of course there are other items he attacks as valid because he attributes certain actions taken as God's order that he personally opposes. He cannot *reason* that God would have such occurrences in His plan. Truly, when all is said and done, there is ultimately an element of faith that one must take. There are many evidences to God, which Paine acknowledges, but in the final analysis, it must all come to our ability to believe. "For by grace you have been saved through faith, and that not of yourselves; *it is* the gift of God, not of works, lest anyone should boast." (Ephesians 2:8-9)

Later in life, Thomas Paine, reflecting on his rejection by so many over the publication of his work (certainly not the reason

---

and Country Encyclopedia of Quotations, (Saint Louis: AmeriSearch, Inc., 2000) 10 to discount it, for there are other reasons for that), is quoted as saying, "I would give worlds, if I had them, if *The Age of Reason* had never been published. O Lord, help! Stay with me! It is hell to be left alone."[60] Faced with imminent departure from this life, Paine stated his last words, "I die in perfect composure and resignation to the will of my Creator, God."[61]

While Thomas Paine held out as an a self-proclaimed deist, many who have been labeled as such would have in no way associated themselves with such philosophy. Those who put their heart and soul into the documents which established and developed this land debated the collective writings extensively. They were not simply the writings of one man in a moment. If you read the documentation of the debates over the Declaration of Independence, the Articles of Confederation, and the Constitution of the United States of America you will find similar activity each time. Nothing was done easily, and nothing was done without considerable time spent on each thought placed into the documents.

The reasons outlined in the Declaration of Independence mirror those expressed in the pamphlet *Common Sense* by Thomas Paine as well as other prominent proposals submitted throughout New England's colonial legislatures.

---

[60] Marshall, Peter and David Manuel, *The Glory of America,* (Bloomington, MN: Garborg's Heart'N Home, Inc. 1991) 1.29 quoted in William J. Federer, ed., *America's God and Country Encyclopedia of* Quotations, (Saint Louis: AmeriSearch, Inc., 2000) 490

[61] Thomas Paine. *The World Book Encyclopedia,* 18 vols. (Chicago, IL: Field Enterprises, Inc. , 1957; W. F. Quarrie and Company, 8 vols., 1917; World Book, Inc., 22 vols., 1989), vol. 13, 6035

The presiding thoughts which drove the colonies toward becoming "free and independent States" were clear: Divine Providence was compelling these colonies to form a Union and separate from England. The reasons presented were due to violations of biblical rights which they were determined to recapture.

One very early founding document issued about the same time as Paine's *Common Sense* is the Constitution initiated by the Commonwealth of Virginia, June 29, 1776. This is within the week before the United States of America declared its own independence. The state constitution began with a list of grievances very similar to that adopted by the United States of America, and then proceeded to outline the rights and government authority. In the Bill of Rights outlined at the beginning of the constitution, the subject of religious liberty is addressed.

> SEC. 16. That religion, or the duty which we owe to our Creator, and the manner of discharging it, can be directed only by reason and conviction, not by force or violence; and therefore all men are equally entitled to the free exercise of religion, according to the dictates of conscience; and that it is the mutual duty of all to practice Christian forbearance, love, and charity towards each other.

The word Christian is prominent in the Bill of Rights Section 16 devoted to religious liberty. In this writing, which sets forth the means of government in the Commonwealth of Virginia, the motivation which pressed those in leadership forward to separation from Great Britain was apparent.

And then there is the State of New Jersey, convening and passing their constitution on July 2, 1776. In it there are religious freedoms granted, and the indication that anyone of any Protestant sect is eligible for election to any office.

> XVIII. That no person shall ever, within this Colony, be deprived of the inestimable privilege of worshipping Almighty God in a manner agreeable to the dictates of his own conscience; nor, under any pretence whatever, be compelled to attend any place of worship, contrary to his own faith and judgment; nor shall any person, within this Colony, ever be obliged to pay tithes, taxes or any other rates, for the purpose of building or repairing any other church or churches, place or places of worship, or for the maintenance of any minister or ministry, contrary to what he believes to be right, or has deliberately or voluntarily engaged himself t perform.

> XIX. That there shall be no establishment of any one religious sect in this Province, in preference to another; and that no Protestant inhabitant of this Colony shall be denied the enjoyment of any civil right, merely on account of his religious principles; but that all persons, professing a belief in the faith of any Protestant sect, who shall demean themselves peaceably under the government, as hereby established, shall be capable of being elected into any office of profit or trust, or being a member of either branch of the Legislature, and shall

fully and freely enjoy every privilege and immunity, enjoyed by others their fellow subjects.

Once again, it is apparent that one particular faith prevailed in the establishment of the state's freedoms and government structure.

The State of Delaware adopted its formational constitution in September of 1776. In it the government officials were compelled to subscribe to the following requirements before assuming office:

ART. 22. Every person who shall be chosen a member of either house, or appointed to any office or place of trust, before taking his seat, or entering upon the execution of his office, shall take the following oath, or affirmation, if conscientiously scrupulous of taking an oath, to wit:

"I, A B. will bear true allegiance to the Delaware State, submit to its constitution and laws, and do no act wittingly whereby the freedom thereof may be prejudiced."

And also make and subscribe the following declaration, to wit:

"I, A B. do profess faith in God the Father, and in Jesus Christ His only Son, and in the Holy Ghost, one God, blessed for evermore; and I do acknowledge the holy scriptures of the Old and New Testament to be given by divine inspiration."

And all officers shall also take an oath of office.

The first line of the Preamble to the Constitution of the State of Pennsylvania read, "WHEREAS all government ought to be instituted and supported for the security and protection of the community as such, and to enable the individuals who compose it to enjoy their natural rights, and the other blessings which the Author of existence has bestowed upon man;..." With this opening Pennsylvania joined itself to the Declaration of Independence in ascribing the idea of a Creator, or "Author of existence". The constitution continues in delineating the rights of the citizenry of the state. In Section II religious freedom is explained.

> II. That all men have a natural and unalienable right to worship Almighty God according to the dictates of their own consciences and understanding: And that no man ought or of right can be compelled to attend any religious worship, or erect or support any place of worship, or maintain any ministry, contrary to, or against, his own free will and consent: Nor can any man, who acknowledges the being of a God, be justly deprived or abridged of any civil right as a citizen, on account of his religious sentiments or peculiar mode of religious worship: And that no authority can or ought to be vested in, or assumed by any power whatever, that shall in any case interfere with, or in any manner controul, the right of conscience in the free exercise of religious worship.

And, as is the case in prior states, the Pennsylvania constitution lays out the requirements of service in its government.

SECT. 10. A quorum of the house of representatives shall consist of two-thirds of the whole number of members elected; and having met and chosen their speaker, shall each of them before they proceed to business take and subscribe, as well the oath or affirmation of fidelity and allegiance hereinafter directed, as the following oath or affirmation, viz:

I do swear (or affirm) that as a member of this assembly, I will not propose or assent to any bill, vote, or resolution, which stall appear to free injurious to the people; nor do or consent to any act or thing whatever, that shall have a tendency to lessen or abridge their rights and privileges, as declared in the constitution of this state; but will in all things conduct myself as a faithful honest representative and guardian of the people, according to the best of only judgment and abilities.

And each member, before he takes his seat, shall make and subscribe the following declaration, viz:

I do believe in one God, the creator and governor of the universe, the rewarder of the good and the punisher of the wicked. And I do acknowledge the Scriptures of the Old and New Testament to be given by Divine inspiration.

And no further or other religious test shall ever hereafter be required of any civil officer or magistrate in this State

Another rather unknown document which had a tremendous amount of influence during the time of America's incorporation is the Constitution of the State (Commonwealth) of Massachusetts. It is the oldest sustained constitution in force. While this document has had multiple amendments to it, the original draft adopted by the Massachusetts Provincial Congress is that which influenced the formation of the Constitution of the United States of America in 1787.

The final paragraph of the Preamble of the Constitution of the Commonwealth of Massachusetts begins with the words:

> We, therefore, the people of Massachusetts, acknowledging, with grateful hearts, the goodness of the great Legislator of the universe, in affording us, in the course of His providence, an opportunity, deliberately and peaceably, without fraud, violence, or surprise, of entering into an original, explicit, and solemn compact with each other, and of forming a new constitution of civil government for ourselves and posterity; and devoutly imploring His direction in so interesting a design, do agree upon, ordain, and establish the following declaration of rights and frame of government as the constitution of the commonwealth of Massachusetts.

What an amazing work! In the very essence of the governmental organization of the State, it was, according to their constitution, the people of Massachusetts who gratefully acknowledged that it was the "Legislator of the universe" (God) in the course of His providence (divine plan) granting them the freedom to be able to establish their legislative activity. And in doing so they "devoutly implor(ed) His direction".

This was primarily written by one who some are trying to refer to as a deist: John Adams. We have dealt with some of Mister Adams' stands on religion previously. Once again, those, including Adams himself, in signing the Declaration of Independence, stated a firm reliance on divine Providence. In this outline of government there is also a suggestion of thanksgiving to God for His guidance.

In "Part the First" of the Constitution, Articles II and III are strongly governed by religious freedom. Article II covers the freedom of worship exclusively, while Article III is devoted to public education. Both are embedded with religious principles.

> Art. II. It is the right as well as the duty of all men in society, publicly and at stated seasons, to worship the Supreme Being, the great Creator and Preserver of the universe. And no subject shall be hurt, molested, or restrained, in his person, liberty, or estate, for worshipping God in the manner and season most agreeable to the dictates of his own conscience, or for his religious profession or sentiments, provided he doth not disturb the public peace or obstruct others in their religious worship.

It is quite clear that each person was open to serve God as they saw fit. They would not be compelled to attend any particular worship service where the government authorized only one denomination.

What is most amazing is Article III. While we are told that it is a violation of someone's constitutional rights to teach the Bible or proffer a prayer in public schools today, the original constitution of Massachusetts outlined that it was to be done so. Not only was there a means by which religious education was to be extended to everyone possible, it was also directed as to which religion would be given preference.

> Art. III. As the happiness of a people and the good order and preservation of civil government essentially depend upon piety, religion, and morality, and as these cannot be generally diffused through a community but by the institution of the public worship of God and of the public instructions in piety, religion, and morality: Therefore, To promote their happiness and to secure the good order and preservation of their government, the people of this commonwealth have a right to invest their legislature with power to authorize and require, and the legislature shall, from time to time, authorize and require, the several towns, parishes, precincts, and other bodies-politic or religious societies to make suitable provision, at their own expense, for the institution of the public worship of God and for the support and maintenance of public Protestant teachers of piety, religion, and morality in all cases where such provision shall not be made voluntarily.

*   *   *

Provided, notwithstanding,...

> ...every denomination of Christians, demeaning themselves peaceably and as good subjects of the commonwealth, shall be equally under the protection of

the law; and no subordination of any sect or denomination to another shall ever be established by law.

Please note that every denomination of *Christians* was outlined in the extended portion of Article III. And this very constitution was approved by the legislature in session along with all other provisions of the document.

Interestingly, "Part the Second" of the Massachusetts constitution outlines the form of government. In "Chapter Two – Executive Power" the office of governor is laid out.

Article I. There shall be a supreme executive magistrate, who shall be styled "The governor of the commonwealth of Massachusetts;" and whose title shall be "His Excellency."

Art. II. The governor shall be chosen annually; and no person shall be eligible to this office, unless, at the time of his election, he shall have been an inhabitant of this commonwealth for seven years next preceding; and unless he shall, at the same time, be seized, in his own right, of a freehold, within the commonwealth, of the value of one thousand pounds; and unless he shall declare himself to be of the Christian religion.

A few of the states, not wishing to have an undue influence of a particular denomination or sect of Christian privilege, prohibited pastors within a denomination to serve in their legislature while acting in an official capacity as a minister. Among those states are those of Georgia, (who required its officials to take an oath "so help me God"), as well as Delaware (mentioned above). Nearly every colony when establishing its statehood and governing constitution clearly indicated their assurance in the Almighty hand of Providence in one form or another.

At the time of the founding of this nation, the predominant ideal was that government could not control a populace without having as its foundation a moral society, substantiated by religious principles and values: Christian values. These values truly formulated the foundations of freedom for the United States of America. ·

Many will look at this and scoff, saying that it is preposterous to think that this nation of freedom would be set up on the very religious foundation that they fight against with every fiber of their being. Yet it is so obvious that at the time of our formation, we were a religious people, and we were primarily Christian. There are those who will point to other documents which state we are not a Christian nation, and these will be observed later.

What cannot be overlooked are the facts. Those persistent and recurring facts that annoy those presenting themselves as atheists, gnaw at the very core of their being. Those stubborn unrelenting facts stare them in the face and they cannot reconcile them in their belief-system.

INDEPENDENCE HALL
Philadelphia, Pennsylvania

In God we Trust

The evidence toward America having a Christian foundation is staggering. The first two centuries which formed the culture of freedom and ultimately led to the colonies declaring themselves a separate nation were inundated with Christian influence. But the Christian experience did not stop at a Declaration of Independence.

The years of revolution which followed were filled with angst at the proposition of war against the greatest, and only true, superpower of the 18th Century. England had just shown its might by emerging victoriously from a war with France and Spain. The spoils of the war included acquiring the territory of the Eastern seaboard of America and the land westward to the Mississippi River, and northward into Canada.

King George III was feeling very confident in the fact that he and his forces, after completing such a major victory to acquire the lands indicated, could quickly quell the uprising by this rabble in New England. The odds were strongly against the colonists, and the talk of independence was strained. The king had pressed his luck too far and he enraged the colonists to a point where the majority, especially those in legislative leadership, were beyond acquiescing any further.

One point that is lost on historical review in many instances is the fact that the Continental Congress had approached the English government, monarchy and Parliament, several times for a redress of grievances. "Olive branches" were extended on more than a few instances. The colonists had done all that could be asked of them, and because of their efforts, English forces were continually landing in greater numbers and exacting the king's vengeance and authority more harshly.

It was in this social and political environment that the Black Robe Regiment was thundering their message in pulpits throughout the land. It was also at this moment in time that the legislatures were calling for a severance of ties to the motherland. It was then that men began to arise and take up arms to protect their families and freedom.

The military "regulars", trained and equipped for war, were a menacing sight to behold. But something gave Americans the courage and stamina to withstand an enemy that appeared undefeatable. It was the same "something" that had caused a young shepherd to enter the field of battle against the

Philistines' mightiest warrior. They had a faith that the God of creation would fight for them.

By the end of 1776, nearly six months after independence had been declared, the revolution was going poorly for the Continental Army. General George Washington had encamped his troops as had the Hessians, and those of England's regulars. In the 18th Century one did not fight war in wintertime. It was unheard of. A skirmish here and there would break out when opposing sides came across one another's path, but battle strategy dictated that a battle in winter was undesirable by either opponent.

It was in this circumstance General Washington and his troops found themselves in December, 1776. Supplies were limited. The men were ill equipped for the winter. Many did not have coats or shoes to endure the weather. The abandonment rate was climbing. And while there had been a few "wins" for the colonials, the defeats were mounting.

Here is where the course of history changed. Almost everyone knows of the great crossing of the Delaware, and the portrayal of Washington leading the charge across the river. The great victory over the mercenary force that day is legend. Against all known logic, Washington ordered the men into battle. And what was it that caused him to do so?

The accounting of what happened has a few versions; however, there is one very good authority upon which to base this as being a true event. The occasion of General Washington seeking the guidance of the one Whom he would later refer to as "that all wise and powerful Being on whom alone our success depends"[62]

According to the description of the occasion, General Washington, immersed in strong concern for the bleak condition in which he found he and the Continental Army, removed himself from the area and found himself a place in which to call out to the Almighty. Deeply engrossed in unrelenting prayer, seeking the direction of the divine hand of Providence in which he trusted, the general was overheard pleading for an answer. It was in this moment that Isaac Potts, working in the forge his brother owned, came across the praying general.

In two different accounts Potts is quoted as recounting the scene. In his talk with Reverend Nathanial Randolph Snowden, an ordained Presbyterian minister, the Quaker tells of his conversion from Tory to supporter of the revolution.

> "I was a rank Tory once, for I never believed that America c'd proceed against Great Britain whose fleets and armies covered the land and ocean, but something very extraordinary converted me to the Good Faith!" "What was that," I inquired? 'Do you see that woods, & that plain. It was about a quarter of a mile off from the place we were riding, as it happened.' 'There,' said he, 'laid the army of Washington. It was a most distressing time of ye war, and all were for giving up the Ship but

---

[62] UShistory.org: *Created and Hosted by the Independence Hall Association in Philadelphia, Welcome to Valley Forge, Washington in Prayer, Washington Avowed God's Blessing,* http://www.ushistory.org/ valleyforge/washington/prayer.html [accessed July 30, 2013]

that great and good man. In that woods pointing to a close in view, I heard a plaintive sound as, of a man at prayer. I tied my horse to a sapling & went quietly into the woods & to my astonishment I saw the great George Washington on his knees alone, with his sword on one side and his cocked hat on the other. He was at Prayer to the God of the Armies, beseeching to interpose with his Divine aid, as it was ye Crisis, & the cause of the country, of humanity & of the world.

'Such a prayer I never heard from the lips of man. I left him alone praying.

'I went home & told my wife. I saw a sight and heard today what I never saw or heard before, and just related to her what I had seen & heard & observed. We never thought a man c'd be a soldier & a Christian, but if there is one in the world, it is Washington. She also was astonished. We thought it was the cause of God, & America could prevail... I turned right about and became a Whig."[63]

The major point to this alleged prayer in the woods is that Washington was well-known as a man of prayer. He was strongly Christian in his actions throughout the war and into his presidency. "Washington offered a day of thanksgiving and

---

[63] UShistory.org: *Created and Hosted by the Independence Hall Association in Philadelphia, Welcome to Valley Forge, Washington in Prayer, Snowden's Diary Gives Data,* http://www.ushistory.org/valleyforge/washington/prayer.html [accessed July 30, 2013]

supplication to his Maker for all of the troops on numerous occasions throughout the entirety of the war."[64]

As his second term of serving as first President of the United States of America came to a close, he offered one of the greatest speeches ever to be brought before the nation on September 19, 1796.

...Citizens, by birth or choice, of a common country, that country has a right to concentrate your affections. The name of American, which belongs to you in your national capacity, must always exalt the just pride of patriotism more than any appellation derived from local discriminations. *With slight shades of difference, you have the same religion, manners, habits, and political principles.* You have in a common cause fought and triumphed together; the independence and liberty you possess are the work of joint counsels, and joint efforts of common dangers, sufferings, and successes.

Of all the dispositions and habits which lead to political prosperity, religion and morality are indispensable supports. In vain would that man claim the tribute of patriotism, who should labor to subvert these great pillars of human happiness, these firmest props of the duties of men and citizens. The mere politician, equally with the pious man, ought to respect and to cherish them. A volume could not

---

[64] UShistory.org: *Created and Hosted by the Independence Hall Association in Philadelphia, Welcome to Valley Forge, Washington in Prayer, Potts' Biographer Speaks,* http://www.ushistory.org/valleyforge/washington/prayer.html [accessed July 30, 2013]

trace all their connections with private and public felicity. Let it simply be asked: Where is the security for property, for reputation, for life, if the sense of religious obligation desert the oaths which are the instruments of investigation in courts of justice? *And let us with caution indulge the supposition that morality can be maintained without religion.* Whatever may be conceded to the influence of refined education on minds of peculiar structure, *reason and experience both forbid us to expect that national morality can prevail in exclusion of religious principle.*

It is substantially true that virtue or morality is a necessary spring of popular government. The rule, indeed, extends with more or less force to every species of free government. Who that is a sincere friend to it can look with indifference upon attempts to shake the foundation of the fabric?

*   *   *

Observe good faith and justice towards all nations; cultivate peace and harmony with all. Religion and morality enjoin this conduct; and can it be, that good policy does not equally enjoin it - It will be worthy of a free, enlightened, and at no distant period, a great nation, to give to mankind the magnanimous and too novel example of a people always guided by an exalted justice and benevolence... Can it be that Providence has not connected the permanent felicity of a nation with its virtue? The experiment, at least, is recommended by

every sentiment which ennobles human nature. Alas! is
it rendered impossible by its vices?

*   *   *

Though, in reviewing the incidents of my administration,
I am unconscious of intentional error, I am nevertheless
too sensible of my defects not to think it probable that I
may have committed many errors. Whatever they may
be, I fervently beseech the Almighty to avert or mitigate
the evils to which they may tend.

*The italicized areas of the above address are for
emphasis.*

In taking his leave of the highest office in the land, President
Washington warned that without moral principles undergirded
by religious (Christian) values it would be impossible to sustain
our nation as truly free. He stated very clearly that with little
variance, the nation all observed the same religious practice
(Christian). And he reiterated that it was the divine hand of
Providence which provides the virtue necessary to be the
nation the United States of America was intended to be.

In developing the prevailing law in this nation, our Founding
Fathers continued the tradition of Christian influence upon
the government. Many have attempted at every point to set
forth the idea that the Constitution of the United States of
America is an atheistic document, devoid of God. In truth,
our republican form of government sustained by a democratic
process is complete in its biblical foundation. Thomas Paine, in
his pamphlet *Common Sense* outlined the reasons of a republic

being the form of government which coincides with principles found in the Bible.

While some states had a requirement of profession of faith in order to serve in their legislature, those outlining the requirements to serve in the federal government chose not to have such a provision. Some read the statement "no religious Test shall ever be required as a qualification to any office or public trust under the United States" to indicate a disfavor toward religion. However, in his article published in the *Connecticut Courant* (Hartford, Connecticut) on December 17, 1787, Oliver Ellsworth described the reasoning behind this being placed in the Constitution. Ellsworth was "an American lawyer and politician, a revolutionary against British rule, a drafter of the United States Constitution, United States Senator from Connecticut, and the third Chief Justice of the United States."[65] He was there while the debates on the articles were occurring, and had an intricate part in drafting the document. Ellsworth explained that the "religious test" had been determined to be a sham in most instances, with such a pledge in God meaning nothing to some.

> If any test-act were to be made, perhaps the least exceptionable would be one, requiring all persons appointed to office, to declare, at the time of their admission, their belief in the being of a God, and in the divine authority of the scriptures. In favour of such a

---

[65] Wikimedia Foundation, Wikipedia-The Free Encyclopedia, *Oliver Ellsworth*. Last modified June 20, 2013, http://en.wikipedia.org/wiki/Oliver_Ellsworth [accessed July 31, 2013]

test, it may be said, that one who believes these great truths, will not be so likely to violate his obligations to this country, as one who disbelieves them; we may have greater confidence in his integrity. But I answer: His making a declaration of such a belief is no security at all. For suppose him to be an unprincipled man, who believes neither the word nor the being of a God, and to be governed merely by selfish motives; how easy it is for him to dissemble? how easy is it for him to make a public declaration of his belief in the creed which the law prescribes; and excuse himself by calling it a mere formality?[66]

The article written by Ellsworth holds quite a few keys to the ideas behind such a reason for stating that there need be no "religious test". In one instance he very clearly points out that one who believes these "*great truths*" may, by some opinion, be less likely to violate the trust committed to him. His point is that these are, indeed, "great truths". On the other hand, he states that one who does not believe in these truths will merely recite the statement and dismiss it as a form of ritual required of him to be able to do what needs to be done.

There is no doubt, however, that the general consensus of those involved in formulating the federal government throughout the revolution, and into the time of the Constitution, were believers.

---

[66]   Oliver Ellsworth, A Landholder, "To the Landholders an d Farmers," *Connecticut Courant,* December 17, 1787.

In the Articles of Confederation, the first agreement between the states to be formally joined in one effort of government, the preamble prominently declared that "The delegates of the United States of America in Congress assembled did on the fifteenth day of November in the year of Our Lord one thousand seven hundred and seventy-seven, and in the second year of the independence of America, agree to certain articles of confederation and perpetual union between the states…"

The word "Our" is truly capitalized in the document, indicating their belief that it was in the year of their Lord. Some would point out that many documents of the era were dated in such a manner; however, it is to be noted that in many of those instances the word "our" was rarely capitalized unless it was being emphasized.

Also noteworthy is the fact that they were very careful to indicate that it was the second year of the independence of America. One thing which must be pointed out is that each phrase, each concept, in these documents presented by the Continental Congress, and the Congress of the United States, were meticulously debated and only those which were agreed upon in session were included.

Referring to this concept it may also be noted that in the Articles of Confederation, the conclusion reads as follows:

> And Whereas, It hath pleased the Great Governor of the World to incline the hearts of the legislatures we respectively represent in congress to approve of, and to authorize us to ratify, the said Articles of Confederation

and perpetual union: Know Ye, That we the undersigned delegates, by virtue of the power and authority to us given for that purpose, do by these presents, in the name and in behalf of our respective constituents, fully and entirely ratify and confirm each and every of the said Articles of Confederation and perpetual union, and all and singular the matters and things therein contained:...

Done at Philadelphia in the state of Pennsylvania the ninth day of July in the year of Our Lord one thousand seven hundred and seventy-eight, and in the third year of the independence of America.

Not only did these in Congress state the year of "Our Lord" and the "independence of America" at the outset of the document, but also by affixing their signatures at the conclusion. It was a determined action.

It may also be observed that the Constitution of the United States of America is also dated by stating very clearly that it was "Done in Convention by the Unanimous Consent of the States present the Seventeenth Day of September in the Year of our Lord one thousand seven hundred and Eighty seven and of the Independence of the United States of America the Twelfth. In Witness whereof We have hereunto subscribed our Names."

The Bill of Rights is comprised of the first ten amendments to the Constitution. In these our founders went beyond the mere establishment of how the government would operate, and laid out those rights which compelled them to independence. The addition of these amendments was critical to the passage of the Constitution.

In the very first amendment several key rights were outlined. And the first of these was the precious right to openly worship God however one would choose.

> Congress shall make no law respecting an establishment of religion, or prohibiting the free exercise thereof; or abridging the freedom of speech, or of the press; or the right of the people peaceably to assemble, and to petition the Government for a redress of grievances.

What many do not realize is that there were originally twelve amendments to the Constitution proposed in 1789, and the first two were rejected by the states having to do with the numbers and payment for representatives. What became the First Amendment was originally the Third. It was this amendment which began to outline the rights of the citizens of the nation, and thereby these were passed within the states.

The First Amendment begins by restricting the ability of Congress to pass any laws which prohibit anyone from freely worshipping God as they choose. The misinterpretation of the "establishment clause" (Congress shall make no law respecting the establishment of religion) has been a focal point of the attack on Christianity. This will be approached later. What becomes clear is the fact that the second clause of the amendment regarding religious freedom is greatly overlooked. It may be stated as "Congress shall make no law... prohibiting the free exercise (of religion)." Just as surely as Congress was denied the ability to establish a particular sect of religion as a "national religion" it is denied the ability to prohibit its free exercise.

Throughout the nation's history, we have trusted in God. From the first step of explorers, and onward to the villages of those seeking religious refuge, God has been with those settling America. As the colonies grew, so did the dependence on God. And when America faced its greatest challenge against the most powerful army in the world, our hope rested in the guiding and protecting hand of divine Providence.

In the Civil War it is told that "In God We Trust" was the battle cry of the 125th Pennsylvania Infantry... on September 17, 1862, during the Battle of Antietam.[67] They appear to have taken this from "The Star Spangled Banner", written during the War of 1812.[68] In 1864 it was determined by Congress that "In God We Trust" would be printed on the coinage of the United States of America. It seems that this action was taken to present to others that God was on the side of the Union forces.

In this land of America much has been said and shown that undoubtedly marks the United States as a Christian nation. Many of our Founding Fathers based their existence and the

---

[67] Wikimedia Foundation, Wikipedia-The Free Encyclopedia, *In God we trust*. Last modified July 28, 2013, http://en.wikipedia.org/wiki/In_God_we_trust [accessed August 1, 2013]

[68] Ibid

ability to face the storm brought on by independence because they had faith in the Almighty.

While *The Battle Hymn of the Republic* is one well-known song among Christian patriots, there is one that captured the American spirit of the Revolution. William Billings, writer of the song, has been called the "father of American music".[69] The tune is tribute to the military fighting against the British Regulars.

Chester

Let tyrants shake their iron rod,
And slavery clank her galling chains;
We fear them not, we trust in God –
New England's God forever reigns.

Howe and Burgoyne, and Clinton, too,
With Prescott and Cornwallis joined;
Together plot our overthrow,
In one infernal league combined.

When God inspired us for the fight,
Their ranks were broke, their lines were forced;
Their ships were shattered in our sight,
Or swiftly driven from our coast.

The foe comes on with haughty stride;

---

[69] Erik Bruun & Jay Crosby, eds. *Our Nation's Archive: The History of the United States in Documents* (New York: Black Dog and Leventhal Publishers, Inc., 1999), 137

Our troops advance with martial noise;
Their veterans flee before our youth,
And generals yield to beardless boys.

What grateful offering shall we bring?
What shall we render to the Lord?
Lord hallelujahs let us sing,
And praise his name on every chord.[70]

What about the aforementioned *Star Spangled Banner*? This is our national anthem, and yet many only know the first verse. The fourth stanza of the song outlines the basis for the freedom of this nation, and Whom is to be praised.

O thus be it ever, when freemen shall stand
Between their loved home and the war's desolation.
Blest with vict'ry and peace, may the Heav'n rescued land
Praise the Power that hath made and preserved us a nation!
Then conquer we must, when our cause it is just,
And this be our motto: "In God is our trust."
And the star-spangled banner in triumph shall wave
O'er the land of the free and the home of the brave![71]

[70] Erik Bruun & Jay Crosby, eds. *Our Nation's Archive: The History of the United States in Documents* (New York: Black Dog and Leventhal Publishers, Inc., 1999), 137

[71] Wikimedia Foundation, Wikipedia-The Free Encyclopedia, *The Star-Spangled Banner.* Francis Scott Key, *The Star Spangled Banner* (lyrics), 1814, Last modified July 16, 2013, http://en.wikipedia.org/wiki/The_Star-Spangled_Banner [accessed August 2, 2013]

THE LIBERTY BELL
Philadelphia, Pennsylvania

One Nation Under God

I pledge allegiance to the flag of the United States of America

And to the Republic for which it stands

One Nation, under God, indivisible, with liberty and justice for all

On January 14, 1969 a comedian by the name of Red Skelton presented his "Commentary on the Pledge of Allegiance" during his variety show on CBS Television. In it he recounted the story of a principle at Vincennes public schools interceding after the Pledge was recited. Each element of the pledge was broken down word and phrase until the entire pledge was explained in wondrous detail, providing insight on the essence of the recitation. He helped those students realize that it is not to be rote that becomes meaningless. Instead, it should be taken to heart each time it is repeated. At the end of the recollection, he made an observation.

> Since I was a small boy, two states have been added to our country, and two words have been added to the Pledge of Allegiance: Under God. Wouldn't it be a pity if someone said, "That is a prayer" -- and that be eliminated from our schools, too?[72]

Mister Skelton voiced the concerns of many who were living during that time. During a recent discussion with a friend of Red, a couple of facts were brought to my attention. Since his monologue in 1969, his "Commentary on The Pledge of Allegiance" has been introduced in the Congressional Record at least twice, and a framed copy hangs in the Oval Office of the White House since the administration of President Richard Nixon.

At the time of the skit, there was a massive movement to remove God from society completely. Those assaulting Christianity said they were fine with others worshipping God to stay in their places of worship, but in truth they continue to strike hard against God wherever He may be found. More of this attack on Christianity will be considered later.

For more than a century and a half the social landscape of America was saturated with references to God. Many scriptures from the Bible were common knowledge. The general populace

---

[72] Red Skelton, *Commentary on The Pledge of Allegiance,* January 14, 1969, The Red Skelton Show – CBS Television, Copyright Lothian Skelton, 2009

could quote many verses beyond John 3:16, which is also becoming less and less prominent in today's environment.

Washington D.C., our nation's capital, is infused with references to the Bible. Within the walls of its various buildings and monuments are inscribed multiple references of Scripture. In the Library of Congress, particularly in its main reading room, are statues engraved representing the various fields of knowledge.

> Moses and Paul represent Religion, with the inscription, "What doth the Lord require of thee, but to do justly, and to love mercy and to walk humbly with thy God." Science is represented by, "The heavens declare the glory of God; and the firmament showeth His handywork." History: "One God, one law, one element, and one far-off divine event, to which the whole creation moves."[73]

Many are not aware that in the top of the Washington Monument at west end of the National Mall in Washington, D.C. are imprinted the words "Laus Deo", or in English translation, "Praise be to God". Also, as one ascends the staircase within the monument, there are several references to scripture engraved on the walls. Phrases such as "Train up a child in the way he should go, and when he is old he will not depart from it", "Search the Scriptures", and "Holiness unto the Lord" are prominent therein.

---

[73] Providence Foundation, Training and Networking Leaders to Transform Nations, In God We Trust: *America's Historic Sites Reveal Her Christian Foundations*. Last modified July 9, 2013, http://en.wikipedia.org/wiki/ Education_in_the_Thirteen_Colonies [accessed August 3, 2013]

To further understand George Washington, General, Commander-in-Chief, and President, we may look at his proclamation for a day of thanksgiving issued January 1, 1795.

When we review the calamities which afflict so many other nations, the present condition of the United States affords much matter of consolation and satisfaction. Our exemption hitherto from foreign war, an increasing prospect of the continuance of that exemption, the great degree of internal tranquillity we have enjoyed, the recent confirmation of that tranquillity by the suppression of an insurrection which so wantonly threatened it, the happy course of our public affairs in general, the unexampled prosperity of all classes of our citizens, are circumstances which peculiarly mark our situation with indications of the Divine beneficence toward us. In such a state of things it is in an especial manner our duty as a people, with devout reverence and affectionate gratitude, to acknowledge our many and great obligations to Almighty God and to implore Him to continue and confirm the blessings we experience.

Deeply penetrated with this sentiment, I, George Washington, President of the United States, do recommend to all religious societies and denominations, and to all persons whomsoever within the United States to set apart and observe Thursday, the 19th day of February next, as a day of public thanksgiving and prayer, and on that day to meet together and render their sincere and hearty thanks to the Great Ruler of Nations for the manifold and signal mercies which distinguish our lot as a nation, particularly for the possession of constitutions of government which unite and by their union establish liberty with order; for the preservation of our peace, foreign and domestic; for the seasonable control which has been given to a spirit of disorder in the suppression of the late insurrection, and generally, for the prosperous course of our affairs, public and private; and at the same time humbly and fervently to beseech the kind Author of these blessings graciously to prolong them to us; to imprint on our hearts a deep and solemn sense of our obligations to Him for them; to teach us rightly to estimate their immense value; to preserve us from the arrogance of prosperity, and from hazarding the advantages we enjoy by delusive pursuits; to dispose us to merit the continuance of His favors by not abusing them; by our gratitude for them, and by a correspondent conduct as citizens and men; to render this country more and more a safe and propitious asylum for the unfortunate of other countries; to extend among us true and useful knowledge; to diffuse and establish habits of sobriety, order, morality, and piety, and finally, to impart all the blessings we possess, or ask for ourselves, to the whole family of mankind.[74]

---

[74] Yale Law School: Lillian Goldman Law Library: In memory of Sol Goldman, The Avalon Project: Documents in Law, History and Diplomacy, http://avalon.law.yale.edu/18th_century/gwproc11.asp, (Accessed August 3, 2013).

At another very famous memorial in the nation's capital, across the Tidal Basin from the Washington Monument, stands the Jefferson Memorial. From there one may view what Thomas Jefferson's statue was placed to see. Across the way, in direct sight of Jefferson and those looking out of the pillars surrounding the memorial, is the White House. On one prominent wall a writing of Jefferson, again noted as one of the figures of American history which was less inclined to a faith in God, is inscribed.

> God who gave us life gave us liberty. Can the liberties of a nation be secure when we have removed a conviction that these liberties are the gift of God? Indeed I tremble for my country when I reflect that God is just, that His justice cannot sleep forever. Commerce between master and slave is despotism. Nothing is more certainly written in the book of fate than that these people are to be free. Establish the law for educating the common people. This it is the business of the state to effect and on a general plan.

This inscription is a summary enjoined of four writings of Jefferson on the concept of slavery. Can it be assumed through this summary of his thoughts that his idea of God was at the very least one which saw Him as genuinely caring and involved in the affairs of mankind, and, particularly, nations whom were blessed by His hand?

Quickly moving to another memorial at the opposite end of the National Mall from the Washington Monument is the Lincoln Memorial. Two great speeches of President Abraham Lincoln are carved into the marble. Both reflect on the Bible for their basis. In his second inaugural, one of those two speeches, he concludes by admitting that both sides in the conflict of the Civil War pray for the sustenance and overcoming power of the Almighty. Having said this he concludes by saying:

> The Almighty has His own purposes. 'Woe unto the world because of offenses; for it must needs be that offenses come, but woe to that man by whom the offense cometh.' If we shall suppose that American slavery is one of those offenses which, in the providence of God, must needs come, but which, having continued through His appointed time, He now wills to remove, and that He gives to both North and South this terrible war as the woe due to those by whom the offense came, shall we discern therein any departure from those divine attributes which the believers in a living God always ascribe to Him? Fondly do we hope, fervently do we pray, that this mighty scourge of war may speedily pass away. Yet, if God wills that it continue until all the wealth piled by the bondsman's two hundred and fifty years of unrequited toil shall be sunk, and until every drop of blood drawn with the lash shall be paid by another drawn with the sword, as was said three thousand years ago, so still it must be said 'the judgments of the Lord are true and righteous altogether'. With malice toward none; with charity for all; with firmness in the right, as God gives us to see the right, let us strive on to finish the work we are in; to bind up the nation's wounds; to care for him who shall have borne the battle, and for his

widow, and his orphan – to do all which may achieve and cherish a just and lasting peace, among ourselves, and with all nations.

This speech was delivered before Congress March 4, 1865. Just a little over a month later, April 9, 1865, General Robert E. Lee would surrender to General Ulysses S. Grant at the Appomattox Courthouse in Virginia. Having received the news of the surrender, President Lincoln went to the theatre the night of April 14, 1865, and was fatally shot by John Wilkes Booth. The President would die the next morning.

Many other buildings, including that which houses the United States Supreme Court, carry upon their façades and within their hallowed halls references to the Bible and prominently display statues of great men and women of faith. The Capitol Building, where both houses of Congress meet, is inundated with such references. The rotunda contains eight paintings by John Trumbull, depicting great events of the nation's history. Of those eight, half of them either depict a religious event or prominently display the Christian cross in the moment of the event. One cannot tour Washington, D.C. without gaining a general appreciation of the biblical aspects of America coming together.

In addition to these proofs of God's prominence in American history, there are further actions taken within the halls of Congress and the Supreme Court which are very difficult for the non-believer to accept. Each of these elements of government has declared such to be true. We have already discussed Presidential proclamations to the effect that the Almighty has had a determining hand in the matters of the United States of America's existence.

A group asking that chaplains be removed from the Houses of the United States Congress as well as the Army and Navy approached the Senate in 1852. The Senate Judiciary Committee issued their report early the following year. After pointing out the various examples of the founders supporting religious activity within the government, they indicated very strongly that they had every right to support chaplains in these areas.

Our fathers were true lovers of liberty, and utterly opposed to any constraint upon the rights of conscience. They intended, by this amendment (the first) to prohibit "an establishment of religion" such as the English church presented, or anything like it. But they had no fear or jealousy of religion itself, nor did they wish to see us an irreligious people; they did not intend to inhibit a just expression of religious devotion by the legislators of the nation, even in their public character as legislatures; they did not intend to send our armies and navies forth to do battle for their country without any national recognition of that God on whom success or failure depends; they did not intend to spread over all the public authorities and the whole public action of the nation the dead and revolting spectacle of atheistical apathy. Not so had the battles of the revolution been fought, and the deliberations of the revolutionary Congress conducted. On the contrary, all had been done with a continual appeal to the Supreme Ruler of the world, and an habitual reliance upon His protection of the righteous cause which they commended to His care.[75]

Similarly, the Judiciary Committee of the House of Representatives was approached by a group requesting that Christianity be removed from all government proceedings in 1853. The committee took a full year in reviewing the request and its findings, presented on March 27, 1854, stated the following:

> Down to the Revolution, every colony did sustain religion in some form. It was deemed peculiarly proper that the religion of liberty should be upheld by a free people. Had the people, during the Revolution, had a suspicion of any attempt to war against Christianity, that Revolution would have been strangled in its cradle. At the time of the adoption of the Constitution and the amendments, the universal sentiment was that Christianity should be encouraged – not any one sect.

> *   *   *

> If there be a God who hears prayer – as we believe there is – we submit, that there never was a deliberative body that so eminently needed the fervent prayers of righteous men as the Congress of the United States.

*   *   *

---

[75] United States Senate: Judiciary Committee Report, *Chaplains in Congress, and in the Army and Navy.* (January 19, 1853).

...we beg leave to rescue ourselves from the imputation of asserting that religion is not needed to the safety of civil society. It must be considered as the foundation on which the whole structure rests. Laws will not have permanence or power without the sanction of religious sentiment – without a firm belief that there is a Power above us that will reward our virtues and punish our vices. In this age there can be no substitute for Christianity; that, in its general principles, is the great conservative element on which we must rely for the purity and permanence of free institutions. That was the religion of the founders of the republic, and they expected it to remain the religion of their decendents.[76]

In the case of *HOLY TRINITY CHURCH v. U.S., 143 U.S. 457, 12 S.Ct. 511, 36 L.Ed. 226,* the Supreme Court delivered its findings on February 29, 1892. Holy Trinity Church in New York City had brought in a minister from England for employ in their congregation. According to a law enacted by Congress, no one was to be able to do so. The court handed down a ruling stating that Holy Trinity Church would be able to do so under their rights as a religious organization. Within the body of the ruling is the following statement.

If we pass beyond these matters to a view of American life, as expressed by its laws, its business, its customs, and its society, we find everywhere a clear recognition of

---

[76] United States House of Representatives: Judiciary Committee Report, *Chaplains in Congress, and in the Army and Navy.* (March 27, 1854).

the same truth. Among other matters note the following: The form of oath universally prevailing, concluding with an appeal to the Almighty; the custom of opening sessions of all deliberative bodies and most conventions with prayer; the prefatory words of all wills, "In the name of God, amen;" the laws respecting the observance of the Sabbath, with the general cessation of all secular business, and the closing of courts, legislatures, and other similar public assemblies on that day; the churches and church organizations which abound in every city, town, and hamlet; the multitude of charitable organizations existing everywhere under Christian auspices; the gigantic missionary associations, with general support, and aiming to establish Christian missions in every quarter of the globe. These and many other matters which might be noticed, add a volume of unofficial declarations to the mass of organic utterances that *this is a Christian nation.*[77]

When considering the rulings of courts through that day in 1892, it is difficult to understand the ability of the Supreme Court in later years to completely ignore the precedent established by these prior rulings. Beginning in 1948, the Court began to infringe upon the rights of religious practice in reinterpreting the "establishment clause" of the first amendment, noting President Thomas Jefferson's reference to the "separation of church and state". It must be noted that President Jefferson's letter in no

---

[77] United States Supreme Court, *Holy Trinity Church vs. U.S.*, 143 U.S. 457 (February 29, 1892).

way attempted to set up the idea that government was not to promote Christianity in any fashion.

John Jay, first Chief Justice of the United States Supreme Court, believed very strongly in the need for a Christian society controlling the Christian government. He is quoted in the following two statements that to sustain a reliance on Christianity is to maintain the freedom fought for and cherished so vehemently by those in his time.

> "*Real* Christians will abstain from violating the rights of others, and therefore will not provoke war. Almost all nations have peace or war at the will and pleasure of rulers whom they do not elect, and who are not always wise or virtuous. Providence has given to our people the choice of their rulers, and it is the duty, as well as the privilege and interest, of our Christian nation to select and prefer Christians for their rulers."[78]

> "No human society has ever been able to maintain both order and freedom, both cohesiveness and liberty apart from the moral precepts of the Christian Religion. Should our Republic ever forget this fundamental precept of governance, we will then, be surely doomed."[79]

---

[78] Jay, William (1833). *The Life of John Jay: With Selections from His Correspondence and Miscellaneous Papers*. (New York: J. & J. Harper), 376

[79] The Heritage Foundation, Loconte, Joseph, *"Why Religious Values Support American Values"*, http://www.heritage.org/research/lecture/why-religious-values-support-american-values, (Accessed August 4, 2013).

Noah Webster, a prominent figure in the Revolutionary War period, and involved in the establishment of the Constitution, was very outspoken about the necessity for Christian morals in the public square, especially in his later years. Known to have been the "Father of American Scholarship and Education", he composed the Blue Back Spelling Book, which helped standardize the American vocabulary and was utilized for five generations of Americans. He also authored a book on grammar, and a reader. He stated his point on Christian influence very clearly.

"In selecting men for office, let principle be your guide. Regard not the particular sect or denomination of the candidate -- look to his character... It is alleged by men of loose principles or defective views of the subject that religion and morality are not necessary or important qualifications for political stations. But the Scriptures teach a different doctrine. They direct that rulers should be men "who rule in the fear of God, able men, such as fear God, men of truth, hating covetousness" [Exodus 18:21]... [I]t is to the neglect of this rule of conduct in our citizens that we must ascribe the multiplied frauds, breaches of trust, peculations [white-collar larceny] and embezzlements of public property which astonish even ourselves; which tarnish the character of our country; which disgrace a republican government"[80]

---

[80] Noah Webster, *Letters to a Young Gentleman Commencing His Education* (New Haven, S. Converse, 1823) 18-19, Letter 1.

And there are many other examples of those in the government who pressed for Christian action. On D-Day, the day that our forces stormed the beaches of Normandy, President Franklin D. Roosevelt greeted the people of the United States in an address and led them in prayer.

> My fellow Americans: Last night, when I spoke with you about the fall of Rome, I knew at that moment that troops of the United States and our allies were crossing the Channel in another and greater operation. It has come to pass with success thus far.
>
> And so, in this poignant hour, I ask you to join with me in prayer:
>
> Almighty God: Our sons, pride of our Nation, this day have set upon a mighty endeavor, a struggle to preserve our Republic, our religion, and our civilization, and to set free a suffering humanity.
>
> Lead them straight and true; give strength to their arms, stoutness to their hearts, steadfastness in their faith.
>
> They will need Thy blessings. Their road will be long and hard. For the enemy is strong. He may hurl back our forces. Success may not come with rushing speed, but we shall return again and again; and we know that by Thy grace, and by the righteousness of our cause, our sons will triumph.
>
> They will be sore tried, by night and by day, without rest-until the victory is won. The darkness will be rent

by noise and flame. Men's souls will be shaken with the violences of war.

For these men are lately drawn from the ways of peace. They fight not for the lust of conquest. They fight to end conquest. They fight to liberate. They fight to let justice arise, and tolerance and good will among all Thy people. They yearn but for the end of battle, for their return to the haven of home.

Some will never return. Embrace these, Father, and receive them, Thy heroic servants, into Thy kingdom.

And for us at home - fathers, mothers, children, wives, sisters, and brothers of brave men overseas - whose thoughts and prayers are ever with them - help us, Almighty God, to rededicate ourselves in renewed faith in Thee in this hour of great sacrifice.

Many people have urged that I call the Nation into a single day of special prayer. But because the road is long and the desire is great, I ask that our people devote themselves in a continuance of prayer. As we rise to each new day, and again when each day is spent, let words of prayer be on our lips, invoking Thy help to our efforts.

Give us strength, too - strength in our daily tasks, to redouble the contributions we make in the physical and the material support of our armed forces.

And let our hearts be stout, to wait out the long travail, to bear sorrows that may come, to impart our courage unto our sons wheresoever they may be.

And, O Lord, give us Faith. Give us Faith in Thee; Faith in our sons; Faith in each other; Faith in our united crusade. Let not the keenness of our spirit ever be dulled. Let not the impacts of temporary events, of temporal matters of but fleeting moment let not these deter us in our unconquerable purpose.

With Thy blessing, we shall prevail over the unholy forces of our enemy. Help us to conquer the apostles of greed and racial arrogancies. Lead us to the saving of our country, and with our sister Nations into a world unity that will spell a sure peace a peace invulnerable to the schemings of unworthy men. And a peace that will let all of men live in freedom, reaping the just rewards of their honest toil.

Thy will be done, Almighty God.

Amen.[81]

God has granted America to be a nation of great victories. The United States of America is a country blessed by prosperity to the extent that while we sorrow at our economic circumstance

---

[81] Franklin D. Roosevelt: "Prayer on D-Day," June 6, 1944. Online by Gerhard Peters and John T. Woolley, *The American Presidency Project.* http://www.presidency.ucsb.edu/ws/?pid=16515 (accessed August 5, 2013)

we still stand above many other nations who would be thankful to be in our condition of success and goods. While we eat food and discard the excess because it does not suit our taste, millions around the globe are starving.

America needs to return to its understanding that we did not come here alone. It is not just the ingenuity found in the heart of an American that gave us the productivity in various aspects of commerce. It is not the bravado alone of our fighting men and women on the field of battle that produced victories where none should have been obtainable. It is the favor, the grace, of God.

Yet there are many who have come out in absolute assault against the God of the Bible, and the God of America. They have taken it upon themselves to attempt to eradicate Him from our marketplace, our educational systems, and our societal interactions. In doing so, and by the Christian's permission of it in accepting the lies perpetrated, we have found ourselves in a most perilous time.

MOUNT SOLEDAD CROSS AND FLAG
San Diego, California

The War Against Christianity

A decade and more into the new millennium, the 21st Century, the nation is reaping the results of a government grown to unmanageable levels and a society uneducated in Christian principles. While many municipalities attempt to implement ordinances that would cut the rising tide of crime, the cause is the battle against immense waves of destructive rebellion within all stratums of society.

The Bible talks of such times as "perilous". A thorough description of a society gone amok without God can be found in II Timothy 3:1-7.

> But know this, that in the last days perilous times will come: For men will be lovers of themselves, lovers of money, boasters, proud, blasphemers, disobedient to parents, unthankful, unholy, unloving, unforgiving, slanderers, without self-control, brutal, despisers of

133

good, traitors, headstrong, haughty, lovers of pleasure rather than lovers of God, having a form of godliness but denying its power. And from such people turn away! For of this sort are those who creep into households and make captives of gullible women loaded down with sins, led away by various lusts, always learning and never able to come to the knowledge of the truth.

Christians must understand that we are living in a challenging time. While each generation has its obstacles and trials to deal with, ours is unique in history. At this time the entire world is connected. The boundaries which separate us are quickly disappearing. Access to knowledge is a fraction of a second away. And equally as accessible is those which can bring someone to spiritual ruin.

When the aspect of immorality is added to the mixture there is a chaotic reaction of anarchy. Literally, a definition of anarchy is a "lack of obedience to an authority, or insubordination"[82]. We certainly live in a day when society in general has become narcissistic in its approach. Most approach life from a standpoint of what is best for them. The idea of a community being of primary concern is foreign to a growing number of individuals.

This did not happen overnight. In fact, this began several thousand years ago in a garden called Eden. Man, created in the image of God, was to be collective in his approach to life.

---

[82] anarchy. Dictionary.com. *Dictionary.com Unabridged.* Random House, Inc.http://dictionary.reference.com/browse/anarchy (accessed: August 05, 2013).

From the very beginning God declared,... "*It is* not good that man should be alone; I will make him a helper comparable to him." (Genesis 2:18) And there is a sense of sharing in a communion with God for the two. "And they heard the sound of the LORD God walking in the garden in the cool of the day,..." (Genesis 3:8).

We do not know how long this time of perfect harmony between God and man continued, but what is known is that it was not long before the attack began. Eve, strolling through the garden, is approached by a serpent near the tree of the Knowledge of Good and Evil. This is the one forbidden item in the garden: one restriction. Only one item in all creation is off limits to Adam and Eve, and only one punishment: death.

The conversation that followed between Eve and the serpent outlines the pattern for Satan's attack throughout history: questioning God and self-centered gratification. The approach to Eve in placing a doubt regarding God's command is, at first, subtle. "Has God indeed said...?", becomes the center-point for the remainder of the conversation.

This is the Enemy's first element of attacking mankind today. It is the basis upon which the struggle between right and wrong, good and evil, truth and lie is fashioned. If God did not create the heavens and the earth, or if *there is no God*, then all other facets of biblical truth have no foundation. And, as the Word of God says, "If the foundations are destroyed, what can the righteous do?" (Psalm 11:3).

The clear attack on Christianity today is one that questions the very existence of God. And where they cannot stop the belief in God, they question the truth of what He has set forth. The concept of Evolution, made popular by the studies and writings of Charles Darwin, is the chief perpetration of that challenge to God and His Word.

These challenges to God and His ability began, as noted, in the Garden of Eden, but they certainly did not stop there. There are multiple times through history where God has been challenged by the reigning authority or predominant social understanding. And this is true even in the founding of America.

As pointed out previously, there were those who have challenged our Christian heritage in the earliest stages of the nation. Thomas Paine, who had used Bible passages to emphasize the need and support for revolution in his pamphlet, *Common Sense*, later questioned the truth of such Scripture in his work, *The Age of Reason.* In addition to Paine, there were others who arose to some status of influence during the late 1700's during a surge of what was called a time of reason, when men began to value their educational prowess over that of their dependence on God. Certain questions of the very existence of God, which have always had their place in the scope of society throughout time, grew more and more prominent. Man, as Lucifer had before the creation of the world, sought to extol himself above any god.

While the notion was mostly dismissed in the late 18th Century, it was gaining in momentum. Many theories began to emerge which supplanted the concept of faith with natural occurrence. Into this emphasis on the natural, and the supposed superiority of science over Scripture, came the theory of evolution.

Perhaps the most destructive of challenges to the authority of the Bible began to gain a foothold with the "elite" in society. The question of "Did God really say?" continued to rise in popularity, chiseling away of the bedrock foundation of the long-held beliefs of the Christian populace. Intellectual reasoning, based on the intellectual pursuits of a human mind set on rationalizing God out of the equation, began to legitimize a world without Him.

While those closest to the events which shaped the United States persisted in proclaiming their reliance on the God of Heaven, and those nearer those truths reiterated them, more lifted themselves up, believing their knowledge to be superior to those before them. Their willingness to disregard prior foundational patterns and to rely instead on their own ability and knowledge drove them to accept anything that would create doubt, as their "father", as Christ put it in John 8:42-45, has done so many times before.

> Jesus said to them, "If God were your Father, you would love Me, for I proceeded forth and came from God; nor have I come of Myself, but He sent Me. Why do you not understand My speech? Because you are not able to listen to My word. You are of *your* father the devil, and the desires of your father you want to do. He was a murderer from the beginning, and does not stand in the truth, because there is no truth in him. When he speaks a lie, he speaks from his own *resources,* for he is a liar

and the father of it. But because I tell the truth, you do not believe Me.

The United States Senate and House Judiciary committees resolutions reviewed previously were direct results of petitions presented to the Senate and House of Representatives respectively by those attempting to remove God from influencing the government. And these resolutions, as well as the Supreme Court ruling of *HOLY TRINITY CHURCH v. U.S.* handed down February 29, 1892, should be precedent for future generations to draw upon. However, when men begin to believe they are more intelligent than their predecessors they tend to ignore precedence.

This is the same mentality that has gained foothold in the intellectual community. They place their "faith" in unfounded theories which more closely align with what they would "hope" to be true. No evidence substantiates their beliefs.

I recently purchased a used copy of Darwin's *The Origin of Species.* I purchased a used copy because I refuse to support the production of any more copies than already have infiltrated our society. I recall being compelled to read this book in high school. I know my children have been taught the theory as fact while as they moved through the public education system. In preparation for my case presented here in this manuscript, I forced myself to stomach reading a great portion of the book once again.

Darwin originally published his book in November, 1859, just two short years before the rumblings of the Civil War turned into a blazing fire of conflict between the Union and the Confederacy. The book which launched a war over creation, even within the church, brought about its own form of divisiveness. Did God do what He said He did? or is there something less glorious that brought about the man-animal to his state of being? The fledgling theory caught wind amongst those desiring to be free from the oversight of a holy God before Whom they would stand and give an account for their actions and beliefs.

In order for Darwin's theory to be true, an intricately complex creature would have to be developed from one independent cell. That cell, of course, is comprised of a complexity of its own in order to sustain its life. Let us take a moment and consider how this would have to occur.

Evolution is the idea that life at some point miraculously sprung from lifelessness, and that life somehow formulated itself over an unimaginable amount of time into variations of life interactive to create one functional cell, which then decided it must actively reproduce itself. Once this group of exacting cells began to interact with the others, each decided, over another unimaginable amount of time to branch themselves into independently functioning interdependent functions which rely each on the other to formulate senses and ultimately produce the multi-celled functional life form with each facet of its being. Each newly formed element now performed its function expertly in a way to sustain the life in its multilevel development.

Then through more time and time and more time it began its development into a multiplicity of interactive creatures and plants which were able to create a functioning atmosphere so that each was dependent upon the other. Some sea creatures remained in the sea, ever branching and developing into more variations which are totally unrelated, and yet sustain certain species at one form. Now we must believe that while gills and such took substance from water, at some point one decided to live above and beyond the water. Once on land, it then branched into creeping, and flight, and climbing and walking upright.

And before we forget to include the true origin of this scheme, we must add that untold eons of time before this something, which must have been something or else it was nothing before it became something, somehow collectively ignited by some unavailable trigger, for no trigger existed; but it had to. This grand explosion, known to science as "The Big Bang Theory", hurled all the appropriate molecules of existence into nothingness and formed into something around the center that was comprised of everything. And somehow on a planet that was perfectly placed a specified distance from a large ball of ignited gasses in a position to where that miraculous initiation of life took place, the process began in begetting life from lifelessness.

I ask you which is more viable? An eruption from nothingness into a grand something that produces life from lifelessness? Or an all-powerful God who formulated each being into the amazing creation it is today? Yes, there are adaptations of species to adjust to their environment. But I propose that this also is a mechanism created by the hand of the Most High.

From where did supposition and thought arise? From where did this being who did not know it had not stopped developing imagine that it should formulate orbs which could develop lenses in a perfect positioning to create sight when a multiplicity of functional interaction takes place?

And, finally, along this line of thought: Why is it that those who know the truth of the Almighty God and His amazing power of creation in six literal days are the only ones called upon to change their viewpoint and adapt it to a theory that has no substantiation?

The study of science teaches us that in the very elemental stage of theory development the scientist approaches his field of study from a preconceived notion that is driven by his innate opinion. Why then is it that the Christian must abandon his or her faith to accommodate an unproven, and unfounded, theory? Is it not the very fact that the atheist scientist is driven to disprove God because he or she approaches the study from their preconceived notion that there is none?

This is where the attack on Christianity becomes more intensive. This is where our faith is forced to withstand the more heated assaults. When those from within our own faith begin to buy into the lie of evolution and of the separation of church and state, it causes those in Christianity to appear divided. While on the other front, those depicting the lies as truth are united in a fervent effort.

"Then the serpent said to the woman, "You will not surely die. For God knows that in the day you eat of it your eyes will be opened, and you will be like God, knowing good and evil." (Genesis 3:4-5) The crux of the second phase of the assault is based on man's desire to "be like God".

> How you are fallen from heaven,
> O Lucifer, son of the morning!
> *How* you are cut down to the ground,
> You who weakened the nations!
> For you have said in your heart:
> 'I will ascend into heaven,
> I will exalt my throne above the stars of God;
> I will also sit on the mount of the congregation
> On the farthest sides of the north;
> I will ascend above the heights of the clouds,
> I will be like the Most High.' (Isaiah 14:12-15)

Mankind was presented Lucifer's original plan to overthrow God. What has brought hatred into his heart is what happened next.

> And (Jesus) said to them, "*I saw Satan fall like lightning from heaven.* Behold, I give you the authority to trample on serpents and scorpions, and over all the power of the enemy, and nothing shall by any means hurt you. Nevertheless do not rejoice in this, that the spirits are subject to you, but rather rejoice because your names are written in heaven." (Luke 10:18-20)

Jesus, by virtue of being God on earth, was able to grant to his disciples the ability to overthrow the works of the enemy, even as God was able to cast Lucifer out of heaven in a moment as lightning. Yet Satan's perseverance continues.

And this is how those bent on the destruction of the acceptance of the Word of God have prevailed. Relentless pursuit of their viewpoint has given them the victory, albeit a temporary one.

Our nation has been force-fed the lie of evolution since the American Civil Liberties Union publicly announced they would represent any teacher who would be accused of violating the law passed in the State of Tennessee which prohibited the teaching of evolution. *The Scopes Trial*, as it is well known, pitted opposing sides of the evolutionary issue against each other. Unfortunately, the church was divided in this case. There were those supposing to be biblical scholars stating that it was entirely possible to include evolution in a biblical framework.

James 3:10 expressly states, "Out of the same mouth proceed blessing and cursing. My brethren, these things ought not to be so." The church should not be dividing in subject matter entirely clear in the Bible. There are other matters clearly outlined which will be dealt with in another area of this writing.

The State of Tennessee had passed a law stating that it was illegal to teach evolution in the public schools. Those wishing to break into the schools, a point from which they could spread their infectious ideology upon the youth of the nation, pursued a challenge to the law as soon as they were presented an opening.

The Bible is the initial element of truth we are given to introduce us to God. By chipping away at the foundation of God's Word, the Devil provides the instability necessary to cause cataclysmic shifts in the faith of those who are not solidified in it enough to defend it. And because of this disease in the body of Christ, the hope of mankind suffers.

The truth is that science supports faith. Faith is one step past the proofs of science. Lee Strobel, a journalist who began as an atheist but came to Christ while trying to disprove divine creation, states, "...the available evidence from the latest scientific research is convincing more and more scientists that facts support faith as never before."[83] His books follow his investigation of the facts of creation, Christ, and other biblical concepts.

In his book, *The New Answers: Book 1*, Ken Ham recognizes the teaching of Christ regarding the creation. "In Mark 10:6 we have the clearest (but not the only) statement showing that Jesus was a young earth creationist," says Ham. "He teaches that Adam and Eve were made at the "*beginning* of creation," not billions of years after the beginning, as would be the case if the universe were really billions of years old."[84]

The questioning of God in these fundamental principles of faith continued past the loss of the case in 1925. After their failed attempts to get God out of Congress and the Military in the reports of the Judiciary Committees and the Supreme Court findings, they did not relinquish their quest for a society without God. By 1948 they had enough clout, and had maneuvered "free-thinkers" onto the Supreme Court in great enough

---

[83] Strobel, Lee, *The Case for a Creator,* (Grand Rapids, Michigan: Zondervan, 2004), 357
[84] Ken Ham, ed. *The New Answers: Book 1* (Green Forest, Arkansas: Master Books; New Leaf Publishing Group, 2006) 28

number to begin their demolition of the Christian society God had blessed for so long.

Ignoring precedent, and creating their own form of law, the Supreme Court finds in *McCollum v. Board of Education Dist. 71*, 333 U.S. 203 (1948) that religious instruction is a violation of the "establishment clause" of the First Amendment to the Constitution. While this had been supported for the preceding one hundred and fifty years by lawmakers from the beginnings of the Constitutional government, they chose to turn their attention away from the facts and find in favor of the rising trend of intellectualism.

From that point forward, there was a persistent loosening of the granite-like principles that had supported this nation for more than one and one-half centuries. With every ruling against God the momentum rose to remove Him entirely from the public square.

In 1961 the Court rules that a Maryland law requiring lawmakers to swear an oath to the existence of God is unconstitutional according to the "establishment clause". Then in 1962, based on the same clause, the Court decides that any prayer conducted in a public school, even non-denominational, is a governmental sponsorship of religion. And in two separate rulings, the Court, in 1963, presents that Bible reading over the public address system as well as having a child engage in reading the Bible in class is a violation of that same "establishment clause". In three short years the Supreme Court of the United States of America rejects fifteen decades of precedent and formulates its own approach to law.

And where is the Church during this time of devastation to the faith principles of our society? They are silenced by the acceptance that there is a "wall of separation" erected between the church and state. The lie of this wall, based on a letter written by President Thomas Jefferson, taken out of context, has been beaten into the mainstream of society by those wishing to eradicate God. And the Church of the modern era, becoming more dependent on their own abilities and education, and less on the God they allegedly serve, questions their own beliefs and withdraws into their community sanctuaries.

Because of the letter written by President Jefferson to the Danbury Baptist Association of Connecticut, one phrase becomes the battle cry of the amoral humanistic element in society. The president was attempting to assure the association that no such assault against their freedom to practice their religion would be permitted. He stated clearly that the first amendment built a wall that would hold Congress back from being able to create another "Church of England" as their ancestors had done across the ocean.

But in the decades of the 1950s, 60s, and 70s, the Church withdrew into their cocoons of solitude, hoping that they would be raptured from the ever-collapsing world around them. It became a concern if a Christian were to dare involve themselves in the realm of politics. The Black Robe Regiment had become the White Robe Retreaters.

More and more attacks against morality and Christianity arose. Abortion, which would have decades before been loudly unacceptable by the Church passed through a Supreme Court determined on wrecking every moral concept they could get their authority to engage.

The society in general continued their pursuit of "if it feels good, do it" mentality in every aspect of life. The unacceptable became acceptable. And America, one nation, under God, fell into the corrupt pit described in Romans 10:20-32.

> For since the creation of the world His invisible *attributes* are clearly seen, being understood by the things that are made, *even* His eternal power and Godhead, so that they are without excuse, because, although they knew God, they did not glorify *Him* as God, nor were thankful, but became futile in their thoughts, and their foolish hearts were darkened. Professing to be wise, they became fools, and changed the glory of the incorruptible God into an image made like corruptible man—and birds and four-footed animals and creeping things.
>
> Therefore God also gave them up to uncleanness, in the lusts of their hearts, to dishonor their bodies among themselves, who exchanged the truth of God for the lie, and worshiped and served the creature rather than the Creator, who is blessed forever. Amen.
>
> For this reason God gave them up to vile passions. For even their women exchanged the natural use for what is against nature. Likewise also the men, leaving the natural use of the woman, burned in their lust for one another, men with men committing what is shameful,

and receiving in themselves the penalty of their error which was due.

And even as they did not like to retain God in *their* knowledge, God gave them over to a debased mind, to do those things which are not fitting; being filled with all unrighteousness, sexual immorality, wickedness, covetousness, maliciousness; full of envy, murder, strife, deceit, evil-mindedness; *they are* whisperers, backbiters, haters of God, violent, proud, boasters, inventors of evil things, disobedient to parents, undiscerning, untrustworthy, unloving, unforgiving, unmerciful; who, knowing the righteous judgment of God, that those who practice such things are deserving of death, not only do the same but also approve of those who practice them.

And the Church, shaking its fist against the darkness, refused to put on the armor of God and wade into the spiritual battle. Instead, it chose to complain about its condition, wondering why children being brought up to believe that they were nothing but evolved creatures resisted authority and chose to believe they knew better than their ancestors.

Nativity displays have been removed from courthouse squares because they "offend" someone. Crosses and symbols of the faith of those who have fought and died to preserve our freedom are being removed or denounced as a violation of the lie of the separation of church and state. Ministers delivering prayers in State Houses of Representatives and Senates are warned not to pray in the name of Jesus. And all the while those in false religions are promoted and praised for support of their heritage.

Jesus warned of such a time when He said, "And as it was in the days of Noah, so it will be also in the days of the Son of Man: They ate, they drank, they married wives, they were given in marriage, until the day that Noah entered the ark, and the flood came and destroyed them all.." (Luke 17:26-27) We are living in that very kind of day.

And what does the Bible say about the day of Noah? Genesis 6:5 explains, "And God saw that the wickedness of man was great in the earth, and that every imagination of the thoughts of his heart was only evil continually."

Today we see those who are charged with the preservation of our nation continuing to challenge its heritage. Even as Israel, a nation founded upon God, and based on His Word, took upon itself a notion of becoming secular and multi-theistic, the United States is, through its leadership, proclaiming that we are no longer a Christian nation.

While societal upheaval occurs around the nation, many prominent political leaders are encouraging a dependence on government rather than God. We are told that we are no longer "a Christian nation".[85] Statistics show that the greater majority of Americans *are* still, indeed, Christian in at least proclamation.

On June 28, 2006, Senator Barack Obama gave a speech in which he chided those who would dare suggest we should hold the Bible as our standard.

---

[85] Senator Barack Obama keynote speech at the Call to Renewal's Building a Covenant for a New America conference in Washington, D.C., on June 28, 2006.

"Which passages of Scripture should guide our public policy? Should we go with Leviticus, which suggests slavery is okay? Or we could go with Deuteronomy which suggests stoning your child if he strays from the faith? Or should we just stick to the Sermon on the Mount, a passage that is so radical that it's doubtful that our own defense department would survive its application? Folks haven't been reading their Bible."

*　　*　　*

"Whatever we once were, we are no longer a Christian nation: at least not just. We are also a Jewish nation, a Muslim nation, and a Buddhist nation, and a Hindu nation, and a nation of non-believers."[86]

On April 6, 2009, President Barack Obama gave an affirmation of what he believed in a joint press conference with Turkish Prime Minister Erdogan.

"We can create a modern international community that is respectful, that is secure, that is prosperous, that there are not tensions… inevitable tensions… between cultures. Which I think is extraordinarily important. That's something that is very important to me. And I've said before, that one of the great strengths of the United States is, although, as I mentioned, you know, we have a very large Christian population, we do not

---

[86] Senator Barack Obama keynote speech at the Call to Renewal's Building a Covenant for a New America conference in Washington, D.C., on June 28, 2006.

consider ourselves a Christian nation, or a Jewish nation, or a Muslim nation. We consider ourselves a nation of citizens who are bound by ideals and a set of values. I think... modern Turkey was founded with a similar set of principles. And yet what we're seeing is, in both countries, that promise of a secular country that is respectful of religious freedom, respectful of rule of law, respectful of freedom upholding these values and being willing to stand up for them on the international stage. If we are joined together in delivering that message, East and West, to the world, then I think we can have an extraordinary impact."[87]

In his message he emphasizes that America is "a secular country that... uphold(s) values, and (is) willing to stand up for them." Where do these "values" come from? How can "values" emerge from anything in a "secular country"? These "values" he is speaking of arose from a republic established on a system of electoral democracy created in a biblical format. Without biblical, or "religious", principles, there is no morality; there are no values. We become a society which does whatever arises in the imagination of their collectively sinful heart. With this type of ideology it is easy to mock the Bible and warp its Scriptural basis.

Paul knew that the Christian had to press forward, and become what God requires us to be so that we may obtain the incorruptible crown. When we stand before Him, and give

---

[87] President Barack Obama in a joint press conference with Turkish Prime Minister Tayyip Erdogan, April 6, 2009.

an account for our lives, and the occurrences that persisted around us, will He be able to say, "Well done thou good and faithful servant"? Or are we going to have to admit that we talked a good game, but were not willing to do what we could to bring our land back to the place it should be? Paul described himself as being all he could be to all that he might win some, and then explained:

> ...this I do for the gospel's sake, that I may be partaker of it with *you.*

> Do you not know that those who run in a race all run, but one receives the prize? Run in such a way that you may obtain *it.* And everyone who competes *for the prize* is temperate in all things. Now they *do it* to obtain a perishable crown, but we *for* an imperishable *crown.* Therefore I run thus: not with uncertainty. Thus I fight: not as *one who* beats the air. But I discipline my body and bring *it* into subjection, lest, when I have preached to others, I myself should become disqualified. (I Corinthians 9:23-27)

In this very moment in time more and more truths the Bible is explicit about in its treatment of lifestyles are under attack. Some churches are joining the side of those proclaiming the sin as righteous. Those who are committed to God in fullness must arise and be counted.

GOD WHO GAVE US LIFE GAVE US LIBERTY. CAN THE LIBERTIES OF A NATION BE SECURE WHEN WE HAVE REMOVED A CONVICTION THAT THESE LIBERTIES ARE THE GIFT OF GOD? INDEED I TREMBLE FOR MY COUNTRY WHEN I REFLECT THAT GOD IS JUST, THAT HIS JUSTICE CANNOT SLEEP FOR-EVER. COMMERCE BETWEEN MASTER AND SLAVE IS DESPOTISM. NOTHING IS MORE CERTAINLY WRITTEN IN THE BOOK OF FATE THAN THAT THESE PEOPLE ARE TO BE FREE. ESTABLISH THE LAW FOR EDUCATING THE COMMON PEOPLE. THIS IT IS THE BUSINESS OF THE STATE TO EFFECT AND ON A GENERAL PLAN.

NORTHEAST INTERIOR WALL OF THE JEFFERSON MEMORIAL
Washington, D.C.

Christian Responsibility

The toll on American morality under the influence of an amoral and vocal minority has been overwhelming. The staggering statistics show that as of this moment, more than 56 million babies have been aborted since the *Roe v. Wade* decision in 1973.[88] As of July 1, 2012, the population of the metropolitan area of New York City, including areas of Pennsylvania, New Jersey, and Connecticut, is nearly 23.4 million. When combined with the population of the greater Los Angeles area, which is 18.2 million, the total is 41.6 million. In order to reach the number of innocents aborted since 1973, you have to add the Chicago metropolitan population of nearly 9.9 million, as well as that of the Denver metropolitan population of 3.5 million.[89]

[88] National Right to Life *Abortions Level Off After Decline* http://www. nrlc.org/Factsheets/FS03_AbortionInTheUS.pdf (accessed August 6, 2013)

[89] Wikimedia Foundation, Wikipedia-The Free Encyclopedia, *List of Combined Statistical Areas.* Last modified April 25, 2013, http://en.wikipedia.org/

The number of unborn children taken forcibly from their mother's womb, and denied the "Life" that is said to be so dear to the United States of America in its Declaration of Independence, would fill four major metropolitan areas across this country, which include the three largest and one which ranks number sixteen on the list.

According to the secular survey, "nearly half of the pregnancies among American women are unintended":[90] Which, in the common vernacular, means "unwanted". This is the crux of the argument for selective abortion. Twenty-two percent of all pregnancies (excluding miscarriages) end in abortion.[91]

There is a common phrase utilized stating that a woman has a right over her own body: that she has a right to a choice. This is a true statement to the extent that she has a right to make a choice regarding her actions, and which activities she allows herself to engage in. The choice is made at the time the conception occurs. Once life has been created, what choice does that forming child have when their mother initiates their termination?

In addition, the sanctity of marriage is being eroded. The established setting for marriage at the point of creation is one man and one woman. "Then the rib which the Lord God had

---

wiki/Table of United States Combined Statistical Areas [accessed August 6, 2013]

[90] Guttmacher Institute, *Facts on Induced Abortion in the United States*. Last modified July, 2013, http://www.guttmacher.org/pubs/fb_induced_abortion.html#1 [accessed August 6, 2013]

[91] Ibid

taken from man He made into a woman, and He brought her to the man. And Adam said: 'This *is* now bone of my bones And flesh of my flesh; She shall be called Woman, Because she was taken out of Man.' Therefore a man shall leave his father and mother and be joined to his wife, and they shall become one flesh." (Genesis 2:22-24)

Again, we are told this is a choice. These individuals are said to want to become a family unit by joining together two men, or two women, into the marital commitment that is intended for a one man / one woman union. This condition of society is described in Romans 10:20-32 as noted earlier.

Before continuing it should be noted that these sins are, indeed, sin. The Bible is very clear about this. It should also be noted that other sin is noted in the Bible, and sin brings separation from God regardless of its extent. "What then? Are we better *than they?* Not at all. For we have previously charged both Jews and Greeks that they are all under sin. - - - for all have sinned and fall short of the glory of God." (Romans 3:9, 23)

At this juncture we find that the gospel of Jesus Christ is what everyone needs. All have sinned, and therefore all need a Savior. The key point is that we have a choice to make as a nation. To continue to be the country we were established to be, and serve the God Who is Creator of the universe, we must return to Him as the Israelites were instructed to do throughout the Old Testament. The United States of America, and its Christian population, will be held accountable for its choices and direction.

In addition to the above statistics showing the rise of those actions God is sorrowed at, churches are closing by the thousands every year. While there are, admittedly, several starting up annually, they are not making up for the losses.

Our children are misinformed to believe that the intellectual pursuits of society are factual, and therefore their parents and/or grandparents do not really know what they are talking about. Because of this, they are turning away from the bedrock principles of morality given by a faith-based education.

Churches today abandon the absolute truth of God's word, becoming social centers, and not soul-saving strongholds of faith. "In spite of the stark example of what happens to churches and movements that untether themselves from absolute truth, there is a similar division occurring within evangelical ranks today. Some believers and their churches are drifting from Scripture to the call of the cultural sirens."[92] God's people need to turn around an realize where their place is in societal influence.

Jesus gave the Church a commandment as He was about to depart this world and ascend into the heavens. His last words to His disciples outlined the critical pursuit they were to engage in, and to us as well. "All authority has been given to Me in heaven and on earth. Go therefore and make disciples of all the nations, baptizing them in the name of the Father and of the Son and of the Holy Spirit, teaching them to observe all things that I have commanded you;..." (Matthew 28:18-20)

---

[92] Jackson, Henry L. and Tony Perkins, *Personal Faith, Public Policy*, (Lake Mary, Florida: Frontline; A Strang Company, 2008), 224

In giving this "Great Commission", Jesus outlined the Christian mission. One key point to remember when considering all that is available to do in reestablishing our nation in its Christian heritage is to remember our primary reason for living the Christian life. The world is lost in a sinful state, and the Christian is to reach out to the lost and lead them to Jesus.

In order to accomplish this, the believer must know their reasons for faith. They must not only know *what* they believe, but *why* they believe it. There are many good books, video sets, and other study materials available on Christian apologetics. Apologetics is not the ability to apologize for one's faith. It is the ability to give solid reason for their faith. Essentially, apologetics is the ability to explain *why* one believes *what* they believe.

It is okay when starting out in our Christian walk to be able to tell others that Jesus has saved us from our sin by His death on the cross. We can explain that all have sinned and come short of the glory of God and that if we confess our sin, He is faithful in forgiving our sin. We can learn the outline of the "Roman Road" (the way the Book of Romans outlines the need to come to Christ for salvation and how we do that). But the Christian must not stop there.

The Church is sent to reach the world through our influence in family, society, and government. In Matthew 5:13-14, Jesus said that we are to be the "salt of the earth" and a "light... on a hill". He then issues a warning, "if the salt loses its flavor", then what good is it? And if the light is hidden, then it does not perform the purpose for which it is lit. In the same manner, if a Christian does not witness to their salvation, and the Savior through whom they have been made whole, then they are not doing as they should, and have become stagnant.

It is imperative that the Church, the Body of Believers, comes out of its hibernation and once again takes its place in prominent influence in our society. With the condition the United States of America is in, it is time for the Christian to follow the commandment of God to His people in turning ourselves back to where we should be.

> When I shut up heaven and there is no rain, or command the locusts to devour the land, or send pestilence among My people, if My people who are called by My name will humble themselves, and pray and seek My face, and turn from their wicked ways, then I will hear from heaven, and will forgive their sin and heal their land. (II Chronicles 7:13-14)

Just as God has outlined the way to salvation through confessing our sin, (repenting of what we have done, which means genuine sorrow; accepting Jesus as our sacrifice for sin, and committing to follow Him the rest of our days), there is also a plan for a people to return to Him as a nation.

The first aspect of the turnaround is to humble themselves. The Christian Church has, in recent decades, decided that it had the answers it needed. Seminars have been conducted to help teach how to give a persuasive talk in luring outsiders into the church building. While there, we are "seeker friendly", attempting to reach them as they wish to be approached. The "hell fire and brimstone" preaching has given way to more gentle assurances. Sin has not been called sin, but the attendant is given opportunity to commit themselves to betterment.

While much of the intensively negative approach was uncalled for, as rules and regulations restricting activity blasted the un-churched away from places of worship, it is equally as destructive to entice the masses into a place where they are not confronted with the real problem of sin. If we are to hold out Christ as a loving Savior, it must be in the context that mankind needs to be saved from something. It is not just a social engineering experiment to adjust the attitudes and actions of someone. Sinners need to be cleansed from their sin by the blood of Jesus Christ.

It is time to go back to God and humble ourselves before Him. Each leader, each congregant, every Christian wherever they serve, must kneel before the Almighty God of heaven and admit that we do not have the answers. One cannot make their own path straight. They cannot overcome the temptations, which approach every person at their weakest point, alone.

The first point of what is known as "The Lord's Prayer" is one of humility. "Our Father in heaven, Hallowed be Your name." (Luke 11:2) The Father is to be acknowledged as having His name, His authority, highly reverenced. It is a name holy above all others. This respect can only come when one realizes how great He is versus how sinful they are. Our nation, as a Christian people, must realize how far down in morality it has been allowed to plummet.

And it is time to pray: not just a "Now I lay me down to sleep" prayer memorized as a child. Those prayers are wonderful in teaching children the importance of time for prayer, but they are not the prayers God is looking for from His people.

True prayer is communication with God. It can be one-on-one, and a very personal experience. But the prayer He is looking for from America is a collective communication in humility begging for forgiveness for the complacency which has prevailed in allowing such immorality to prevail among the populace. While the blame would easily be placed on others, the truth is that the Church is at fault.

"No weapon formed against you shall prosper, And every tongue *which* rises against you in judgment You shall condemn. This is the heritage of the servants of the LORD, And their righteousness *is* from Me," says the LORD." (Isaiah 54:17)

If the Body of Christ remains faithful to their duty to be salt and light they cannot fail. The believers have overcome the world because Christ has overcome the world.

It is no wonder that our Founding Fathers declared times of prayer and fasting when faced with insurmountable odds. They set great example when they called for days of celebration to God for His mighty assistance in the victory. It is this example that must be followed today. This must not be done just once a year on the National Day of Prayer, but regularly, and with earnest heart. Yes, this day should be observed, but in order to bring about the change America groans for, it must be a consistently intensive crying out to God for forgiveness and direction.

And this direction comes when we "seek (His) face". The related story of General George Washington praying at Valley Forge exemplifies the magnitude of what may be accomplished when God's favor and direction are entreated. Christian America needs a directive from heaven. In order to be able to receive this guidance, the collective ear of God's people needs to be open to hear His voice. It is important for each Christian to be where God wants them to be, and doing what He has planned for them.

And how will the Church find Him? "…you will seek the LORD your God, and you will find *Him* if you seek Him with all your heart and with all your soul." (Deuteronomy 4:29) Jeremiah 29:11-13 further explains the ability to find God's will: "For I know the thoughts that I think toward you, says the LORD, thoughts of peace and not of evil, to give you a future and a hope. Then you will call upon Me and go and pray to Me, and I will listen to you. And you will seek Me and find *Me,* when you search for Me with all your heart."

Jesus further reiterated the point by saying, "So I say to you, ask, and it will be given to you; seek, and you will find; knock, and it will be opened to you. For everyone who asks receives, and he who seeks finds, and to him who knocks it will be opened." (Luke 11:9-10)

Once the Church has approached God for His will, the final, and most critical point in proving the desire to return to Him with a full heart and effort is to "turn from their wicked ways." It is the Body of Christ who must turn around from the direction they are traveling. It is with necessity that they should realize their apathy has led them to lose the influence they are destined to have. When God's people turn, it begins a quaking in the spiritual realm that the forces of hell cannot help but sense.

This is where the impact is felt. Before the Church begins to have a true influence on the status of the natural world, it must invoke the authority it holds through the blood of Jesus Christ and the power of the Holy Spirit in the supernatural world.

Paul explains this very clearly when he says, "...we do not wrestle against flesh and blood, but against principalities, against powers, against the rulers of the darkness of this age, against spiritual *hosts* of wickedness in the heavenly *places."* (Ephesians 6:12)

If the Church is to bring down the superstructures built by the forces of sinful existence, it must be done with a revival within the Body of Christ. And the first battlefield must be in a spiritual realm. "For though we walk in the flesh, we do not war according to the flesh. For the weapons of our warfare *are* not carnal but mighty in God for pulling down strongholds, casting down arguments and every high thing that exalts itself against the knowledge of God, bringing every thought into captivity to the obedience of Christ, and being ready to punish all disobedience when your obedience is fulfilled." (II Corinthians 10:3-6)

The call to action for the 21st Century believer is not that of muskets, cannonballs, machine guns, fighter jets, or aircraft carriers. It is not a ground assault to secure the buildings of the nation's capital. This is a day for action: action in the supernatural.

When one gets themselves to the point where they are actively engaged in the heavenly kingdom, they become readied to take action in the natural. God has a plan. He has demonstrated that fact in His Word. It is both an individual and a collective plan. And that plan involves every Child of God on planet earth.

Is any one person, new born Christian or seasoned saint, perfect? Absolutely not. Have any on this planet arrived at the place where they are without error? No. But here is the amazing truth: God has worked in the lives of imperfect humans throughout the course of history and has brought about His magnificent will by their obedience. It is because of this that God declares in I Samuel 15:22, "Behold, to obey is better than sacrifice, *And* to heed than the fat of rams."

Yes, it is important for the Christian to be involved wherever they are led to pursue; in politics, in community awareness, in standing against the wickedness about us on all sides. However, it is most important that we are obedient.

God's people must be willing to do the uncomfortable, and be willing to be an offense at times. It may not be popular, but it is expedient. Mankind must be confronted with the need for a Savior. In order to know they need a Savior, they must know they are a sinner.

There is a critical necessity for the people of God to assess their faith. Is there an Almighty God in heaven able to create the world in six literal "evening and morning" days? Could He have maintained the human race through an ark built by a man to house his family and every land animal on the planet? Did

He part the Red Sea and allow the children of Israel to escape Egypt by walking across on dry ground, and using the same sea to crush the pursuing army? Was He on earth in the form of man as Jesus Christ? Does He still hear and answer prayer? Will He still speak to any man, woman, or child who opens themselves to His will?

In addition to these questions, is He holy? Does He still expect mankind to come to know Him in a personal relationship through Jesus Christ Who died on a cross for our sin, raised from the dead, and has ascended into heaven to prepare a place for His people and serve as intercessor for His people? Is mankind still under the mandate to come to open themselves to the service of God through the power and presence of the Holy Spirit?

Edmund Burke, an Irish statesman and political theorist among other things, is quoted as saying, "The only thing necessary for the triumph of evil is for *good men to do nothing.*" The United States of America is seeing this statement to be true. The time has come for God's people to do something.

There are those who have been working this cause for several years now. Their message is edging its way into the Christian mainstream. It is time for Christians to set aside those minor details of faith which divide us and focus together on the Lordship of Jesus Christ. It is time to unite as one voice to set the biblical morals and ethics specifically outlined in God's Word before the people of the nation. Jesus is "…the way, the truth, and the life." No one comes to the Father except by His sacrifice. No one gains heaven through any other path.

The Church has a responsibility, individually and collectively, to have an impact on the world around them. It begins with a witness to the fact that Jesus is Savior of their life. It proceeds from there. To have an impact on society, the Christian has many options, especially in the United States of America.

Scripture tells us that we do have a responsibility to interact and make a difference in the society we are placed. Paul writes to Timothy and encourages him in the proper approach to those in authority. "Therefore I exhort first of all that supplications, prayers, intercessions, *and* giving of thanks be made for all men, for kings and all who are in authority, that we may lead a quiet and peaceable life in all godliness and reverence." (I Timothy 2:1-2)

The Child of God is compelled to pray for those in authority in the various aspects of prayer. Supplications ask for God to supply needs, Prayers approach God to invoke His authority over the matters of man. Intercessions are prayers on the behalf of another, and can be asking forgiveness on their behalf or seeking God's action for them. And giving of thanks is as it sounds, thanking God for them. Each of these are to be aspects of the Christian's prayer on behalf of all mankind, including those in authority.

Further, there is specific instruction on how the believer is to approach government authority. Once again, it is Paul writing. In his letter to the Romans, who were located at the very center of the Empire's seat of control, and being pursued, beaten, and even killed in the most horrible ways, Paul encourages them to maintain a Christian nature.

Let every soul be subject to the governing authorities.
For there is no authority except from God, and the
authorities that exist are appointed by God. Therefore
whoever resists the authority resists the ordinance
of God, and those who resist will bring judgment on
themselves. For rulers are not a terror to good works,
but to evil. Do you want to be unafraid of the authority?
Do what is good, and you will have praise from the
same. For he is God's minister to you for good. But if you
do evil, be afraid; for he does not bear the sword in vain;
for he is God's minister, an avenger to *execute* wrath on
him who practices evil. Therefore *you* must be subject,
not only because of wrath but also for conscience' sake.
For because of this you also pay taxes, for they are
God's ministers attending continually to this very thing.
Render therefore to all their due: taxes to whom taxes
are due, customs to whom customs, fear to whom fear,
honor to whom honor. (Romans 13:1-7)

It is important to keep in mind that this is written to a people
who are subject under a government who ruled over them in a
society where the Jew was a subject, as was most of the world.
It was not God's government that prevailed as it did when there
was a king over Israel established by God Himself. God held
His chosen people to be responsible for their choices. When
they would reject Him and His direction; when they would allow
other gods to be worshipped in their land and sinful action to
prevail; He would bring them under judgment.

America is a nation established by God and founded upon
Christianity. As a Christian nation, regardless of what others

may say, it will be held accountable for the choice in its course. Believers are to live peaceably while standing our ground on righteous living. The government was formulated for Christians believing religious values and morals must guide our future.

John Adams had an opinion on the critical nature of religion in America. His feelings were quite strong as he issued a letter to a group of military officers.

"…we have no government, armed with power, capable of contending with human passions, unbridled by morality and religion. Avarice, ambition, revenge and licentiousness would break the strongest cords of our Constitution, as a whale goes through a net. Our Constitution was made only for a moral and religious people. It is wholly inadequate to the government of any other."[93]

In addition to John Adams, his wife, Abigail, had an opinion on such matters as well.

"A patriot without religion in my estimation is as great a paradox as an honest Man without the fear of God. Is it possible that he whom no moral obligations bind, can have any real Good Will towards Men? Can he be a patriot who, by an openly vicious conduct, is undermining

---

[93] John Adams Letter to the Officers of the First Brigade of the Third Division of the Militia of Massachusetts, 11 October 1798, in Revolutionary Services and Civil Life of General William Hull (New York, 1848), 265-266

the very bonds of Society?... The Scriptures tell us "righteousness exalteth a Nation."[94]

What is this Scripture that Abigail Adams is quoting? That is in the Bible? Yes. Proverbs 14:34 says exactly that, and more. "Righteousness exalts a nation, But sin *is* a reproach to *any* people."

Joel 3:1-17 speaks of the time when the Messiah will rise up and judge the nations based on how they have treated His people Israel. Nations shall stand before the Almighty and give an account in judgment. God has judged Israel when they abandoned their faith in deference to other gods. God will judge America if it fails to return to Him soon.

Each Christian needs to realize the essential nature of their choices in elections and in pursuing their citizenship in this nation. The believer should know that they are set where they are for a purpose. There is a plan, and that plan is a perfect one.

Many have said that Jesus would not support His people involving themselves in the political process. They try to say that such involvement is against our spiritual reasoning.

Yet Jesus' strongest actions took place in an attempt to bring attention to the corruption of those "in charge". He overthrew the moneychangers' tables and exclaimed that they had turned His Father's house into a "den of thieves" (Matthew 21:13) It is time for God's people to enter the halls of the congresses throughout

---

[94] Abigail Adams to her friend Mercy Warren, November, 1775

our nation, from the national to the varied states, and even into the governing bodies of counties, cities, townships and bergs. It is time to turn over some tables in a spiritual and societal sense.

America has realized the blessings of God in abundance beyond its greatest dreams. As mentioned previously, this country has experienced the most increase of any other land across the planet. Even the poorest of the citizens of these United States of America appear wealthy to a majority of the remainder of the planet. They have been allowed to continued prosperity based on their heritage.

But God will not withhold His wrath forever. I tremble along with President Thomas Jefferson when I realize that God is just, and will not restrain his anger in bringing judgment to a nation who knows better. America IS a Christian nation; and we will be judged accordingly.

The time has come for His people to rise up and take their rightful place in this land. Each Christian can take part in resisting the onslaught of evil. There is a right and wrong. There is an absolute truth. You and I will be held accountable individually and collectively for our actions or lack thereof.

And into this mixture of societal influence God has placed you. As you read this, God has something special in store ahead. With all the adversity being experienced, God has trusted you and your Christian experience to influence your world. Whether it be to touch those in your immediate family, your community, your town, city and county, your state, or the nation, you are being called into active duty. And the question becomes not if, but what you should do. Our Founders set up a nation to be ruled by a people of moral virtue. It has been continued throughout the decades since by men and women purposed to preserve the freedom of that nation. And now... It is your turn!

AT THE SITE OF THE BOSTON MASSACRE
Front of the Old State House
Boston, Massachusettes

It's Your Turn

Nine score and seventeen years ago, our fathers brought forth on this continent a new nation, conceived in liberty and dedicated to the proposition that all men are created equal. Now we are engaged in a great social conflict, testing whether that nation or any nation so conceived and so dedicated can long endure. The conflict is not over land ownership, or to break away from the government set forth by those fathers. This struggle is for the hearts and minds of every man, woman, and child. The outcome of this effort will determine the success or failure of the Great American Experiment.

And right into the middle of this turmoil God set you. You did not choose to be born at this time. You were not consulted as to what your part would be. But your being here at this moment in time and in this place on earth is part of a greater scheme. As a believer you need to know this: you need to believe this.

It is approximately 480 B.C. and the Jews are a people of captivity in Babylon. The Queen of the Empire conducts an act of rebellion against her husband's will, and she is executed. The time comes for a new queen. Esther, a beautiful young Jewish lady, is selected to be the next queen at the king's side. She knows how the previous queen died.

Circumstances around her become very uneasy. One of the king's top advisors, Haman, compels the king through a series of deceitful means to sign an execution order to be conducted against the entire populace of the captive Israelis. Being an Israelite puts Esther in a precarious situation. She is not a revolutionary, and she would like to keep her head, literally.

Mordecai, Esther's uncle who raised her, communicates with her and explains the dire situation. She realizes the circumstances, but states very clearly that she has not been called before her husband in some time, and there is a penalty for appearing uncalled and unannounced. It is then that Mordecai sends a message to Esther... and to God's people throughout history: "...if you remain completely silent at this time, relief and deliverance will arise for the Jews from another place, but you and your father's house will perish. Yet who knows whether you have come to the kingdom for *such* a time as this?" (Esther 4:14) What Mordecai was saying to her is, "It's your turn."

Leap forward 2,500 years. It is a new millennium. Great technological advances have come into the world. A new age of education and knowledge has arisen like never before in the history of mankind. Intellectualism has replaced theological study. That which has been considered wrong for millennia is now becoming acceptable in light of the "new understanding". It is a time very uncomfortable for the Christian. Even those who are supposed leaders of "the faith" are explaining away doctrines held dear by every generation of believers before. And here you are.

You know full well that if you decide to take a stand and voice your faith in the undeniable truths of God's Word you are going to be ridiculed. You know that when you refuse to bow to the idol at the playing of the music you will be looked upon by some you are closest to as though you have lost your mind. Others will feel uncomfortable around you because they think you look at them in a derogatory fashion; when all you are trying to do is help them see their need for Jesus Christ as their Savior.

You look around and view the country you have come to appreciate, love and cherish, and know that it is headed down a path that it must not continue on. At first you contemplate that surely God has someone else who can rise up and make a statement. But deep down inside you feel that tugging to do "something".

This is not an attempt to push a particular doctrine of faith that is not precisely spelled out in God's Word. This is in no way a nudge to get you to step outside the areas of Christianity that you are not completely assured of. But there are scriptures which outline lifestyles and activities that are completely abhorrent to the practices of a Christian people.

So you say to yourself, "But, I'm just (fill in your name here) from (fill in your hometown or state here). What can I do?" A very close friend of mine likes to say to anyone who says, "But I'm just...", "Never justify your buts." And I add to that statement, "You are a Child of the Living God. You have whatever it takes to do whatever it is that God has placed you here to do. You do not have to be a Reverend Billy Graham, a General George Washington, a President Abraham Lincoln, or any other such person you highly respect."

God has taken the most unlikely persons throughout time and turned them into heroes. He took fishermen, tax collectors, and other seriously flawed persons and created a dynamic group of world-changers. He has taken a young shepherd and defeated a giant. He has taken a man wanted for murder from the back side of the desert and sent him back to the land he had fled many years earlier to lead a nation to freedom. He took an obscure young woman and caused her to give birth to the Son of God.

And not one of these had any idea who they were to be when they were called out from their casual lives. They were simply ready to be used, although rather reluctantly in some cases. You are that person today. It's your turn!

So how can you become involved? What should you do? Where do you begin?

There is a starting point that is similar for everyone wishing to engage in God's plan. He tells Jeremiah, "Before I formed you in the womb I knew you; Before you were born I sanctified you; I ordained you a prophet to the nations." (Jeremiah 1:5) God's plan for you began before you were ever conceived. You are unique and special in the eyes of your Creator.

The next step in finding your place is to be attentive to the voice of God. Isaiah's story begins as he is in prayer. Isaiah chapter six tells of his time in meditation in the year that King Uzziah died. He suddenly finds himself in the very presence of God, before the throne of heaven. As Isaiah falls to his face, he cries out that he is not worthy to be in this holy place. He admits, "...I *am* a man of unclean lips, And I dwell in the midst of a people of unclean lips;" (Isaiah 6:5) God dispatches an angel to take a coal from the altar and place it against his lips, sanctifying him for service. It is then that God asks, ""Whom shall I send, And who will go for Us?" (Isaiah 6:8) Now cleansed and ready, Isaiah offers himself to be used, saying, "Here *am* I! Send me." (Isaiah 6:8) God immediately begins to tell Him the plan for his life, what he will say, and what awaits him.

In November, 2008, Tammy Crawford, the worship leader for our congregation, was given a word from the Lord. In her writing dated the fifth of November, she shared that God spoke to her saying, "I Am in control, this is a new day I have brought forth, a new beginning for my people to unite as warriors, to bring forth my word to all who will listen, to unite in intercession as never before. I have opened a door and am preparing the way for those who keep my commands."[95]

She had awakened that morning with a heavy heart from the events and circumstances occurring in the nation. She had reached a crisis point in her experience with God and was questioning why America had come to the point where

---

[95] Tammy Crawford in an open letter to Peakview Church of God, Colorado Springs, Colorado: November 5, 2008. Used by permission.

they would choose the positions of immorality and personal satisfaction as described previously. The Holy Spirit led her to write, "Everyone is speaking their own opinions right now and not listening to GOD! Don't let your thoughts and your own points of view hinder you from what GOD wants to say. GOD is in charge, He has known what was to take place since the beginning and HE knows exactly what is going to take place (in the future)."[96]

God is laying a strong burden on many hearts to get back into the fight. There are many levels of involvement across a wide range of opportunities available to anyone wishing to enter into action. Both spiritual and physical service is open for the believer.

The Founders of our country probably were not thinking early in their lives, *'I will rise up and be involved in a revolution against England.'* Someone had to do something. They were placed in the kingdom for such a time, and they answered the call. Now... It's your turn.

Spiritual Warfare

Perhaps one of the most neglected areas of service is that of spiritual warfare. When Paul writes to the Ephesian church, "Put on the whole armor of God" (Ephesians 6:11), he is not suggesting a physical experience. In context, he is asking

---

[96] Tammy Crawford in an open letter to Peakview Church of God, Colorado Springs, Colorado: November 5, 2008. Used by permission.

each believer to become involved in the spiritual conflict, as is their duty.

> Finally, my brethren, be strong in the Lord and in the power of His might. Put on the whole armor of God, that you may be able to stand against the wiles of the devil. For we do not wrestle against flesh and blood, but against principalities, against powers, against the rulers of the darkness of this age, against spiritual *hosts* of wickedness in the heavenly *places.* Therefore take up the whole armor of God, that you may be able to withstand in the evil day, and having done all, to stand. (Ephesians 6:10-13)

And what does it mean to "stand"? The Greek word for stand in this scripture is histemi (his'-tay-mee, ἵστημι): to stand ready, stand firm, and steadfast.[97] Essentially, the word here indicates we are to be ready to maintain our ground. The idea is to be certain and not retreat. James 4:7 tells the believer to, "…submit to God. Resist the devil and he will flee from you." In order to do so, we must take on the *whole armor* of God.

The spiritual battle begins with a spiritual focus. To take on the whole armor of God is to connect with the One who issues the suit. Every part of the warrior's outfit is achieved by spiritual means. Prayer is the key. The Christian prepares themselves for battle by seeking a closer walk with God. When we do that,

---

[97] Bible Hub by Biblios, *histemi, Strong's 2476,* http://biblesuite.com/greek/2476.htm,

God honors that effort and grants us the protections the Spirit affords us.

Once acquiring the necessary armor, the believer may take their place in the lineup. They may stand their ground. With the mind, heart, soul and actions covered and ready, the saint of God now is ready to engage the enemy.

The reason we are to pray for our families, our friends, those others in the world, and our leaders is so they will be drawn by God to live their lives and conduct themselves in the manner He wishes. God has chosen prayer as the means by which His will is enacted. When we agree upon anything in His will, it is done. We have the power, through prayer, to bring down the enemy's strongholds, as stated very clearly in II Corinthians 10:3-5.

> For though we walk in the flesh, we do not war according to the flesh. For the weapons of our warfare *are* not carnal but mighty in God for pulling down strongholds, casting down arguments and every high thing that exalts itself against the knowledge of God, bringing every thought into captivity to the obedience of Christ...

C. Peter Wagner wrote several books in *The Prayer Warrior Series.* In his book, *Warfare Prayer,* he describes the power of praying in a way which challenges the forces of hell by saying, "Spirit-directed prayer opens the way for the blessings of the Kingdom of God to come upon the earth with healings, deliverances, salvation, holiness, compassion for the poor and oppressed, and the fruit of the Spirit. Above all, God is glorified, worshiped and praised."[98] It is the prayer of the child of God engaged in the struggle that overcomes the world. It is this type of prayer that brings down strongholds. But it is not a "Now I lay me down to sleep" prayer.

A documented "failure" of the disciples is found in Mark 9:14-29. Jesus approaches His disciples and sees a large crowd gathered around them. When He asks what all the commotion is about, a father speaks up and explains that he has brought his son who has "a mute spirit" for healing, and the disciples attempted to engage the evil spirit involved.

At this junction I can see Jesus shaking His head and saying, "O faithless generation, how long shall I be with you? How long shall I bear with you? Bring him to Me." (Mark 9:19) He is brought to Jesus, and it is determined that this evil spirit has attempted to take the young man's life many times by causing him to place himself in extensive danger. Jesus delivers what is a most encouraging word when he says to the father, "If you can believe, all things are possible to him who believes." (Mark 9:23) This promise resonates with us to this day.

Like the young man's father, we have doubts and concerns as to just how strong our faith is. We say along with him, "Lord, I believe; help my unbelief!" (Mark 9:24) One of the most challenging of circumstances is this idea of faith and belief. As Christians we believe in God and know that He is able. Many

---

[98] Wagner, C. Peter, *Warfare Prayer: How to seek God's power and protection in the battle to build His kingdom*, (Ventura, California: Regal Books, 1992) 28

times we have full assurance within ourselves that God is able to do what needs to be done. It is the doubt of ourselves that causes us angst. And this is why this young man's dad begs Jesus to "help (his) unbelief". We must take these concerns to Christ as well.

God has a plan for you, and He knows you can do whatever He has asked you to. The great obstacle that must be overcome is our willingness to step out by faith and say, "Yes, Lord. Here I am. Send me."

What you deal with in these moments is so wonderfully described in what has become one of my favorite songs, "Voice of Truth", by Casting Crowns. I have gathered strength from these lyrics more times than I can count. The message describes being faced by the waves of the sea as we are called by Jesus to exit the boat to come to him, and the giant we face when stepping onto the field of battle when everyone else stays behind in fear. As we consider stepping out to face the fear, the waves and the giant call to us, reminding us how our failures have stopped us in previous efforts. They laugh at us, mocking us, and attempt to elicit a resistance to moving in the direction God has for us. They keep drilling the words into our mind, "…you'll never win… you'll NEVER WIN!"[99] We want to stay behind with the others in their *relative safety.*

The song continues through the chorus which states that all that is being done for God's glory. It is the bridge of the

---

[99] Casting Crowns, *Voice of Truth* by Mark Hall and Steven Curtis Chapman, © 2003, Beach Street Recordings

song which gives a glimpse into how God works through His people.

> ...the stone was just the right size to put the giant on the ground
>
> And the waves, they don't seem so high from on top of them looking down
>
> I can soar with the wings of eagles when I stop and listen to the sound of Jesus singing over me[100]

The difficulty comes when the enemy calls out our name and laughs at us. He reminds us how flawed we are. There are few that have the confidence as a Christian to stand up and say, "I'm the one! Yes! Let's do this!" without first realizing just how human we really are. We have been taken out of lives of sin. We have fallen since we became a believer. We have fought the deepest temptations that, many times, no one else realizes except, perhaps, our closest confidants.

And in the midst of this understanding God calls us to step out and do something extraordinary: to believe that not only He can, but that He will through us. He will make the stone the "right size" and cause it to fly true to the only spot on the giant's forehead where it will do the most damage. And He will empower us through the Holy Spirit to be able to have the faith to step out of the boat and realize that when it comes to the

---

[100] Casting Crowns, *Voice of Truth* by Mark Hall and Steven Curtis Chapman, © 2003, Beach Street Recordings

perilous circumstances that seem to surround us, "even the winds and the sea obey Him." (Matthew 8:27)

The Bible says, "And He Himself gave some *to be* apostles, some prophets, some evangelists, and some pastors and teachers, for the equipping of the saints for the work of ministry, for the edifying of the body of Christ". (Ephesians 4:11-12) So there are some who might interject that it is up to these *leaders* to work the mission.

But the Scripture specifically points out that one of the purposes of these leaders is for the "*equipping of the saints for the work of ministry.*" The leaders must be at work in their role to make the believers ready by training them in the cause and work of Christ, but then it is the responsibility of the Christian to take their place in the plan. It's your turn.

To prepare yourself spiritually is to be humble, pray, seek God's help and guidance, and place yourself where He can use you. And at the conclusion of the story in Mark chapter nine, Jesus says that in order to battle on a spiritual plane effectively the believer must be able to pray and fast.

Without going into a great amount of detail on fasting, suffice it to say that the essence of doing so comes from our denying ourselves of our desires for a time in order to completely focus on God and His purposes. Most of the time fasting refers to food, but God may impress you to fast from watching television, if you do so, or other activity to place yourself in a position to use the time you would normally be involved with that activity to build your relationship with Him and open yourself to hearing what He has to say.

Our efforts must begin on a spiritual level. Without the foundations of a deep and meaningful relationship with God, anything else is mere activity. But when your involvement in what He is calling you to do is undergirded with the spiritual power of God, there is nothing that is outside His ability to see it come to pass. The weapons of our warfare are spiritual. And they are MIGHTY THROUGH GOD! Strongholds of the enemy... prepare to fall!

Which Path?

The great question which concerns many Christians once they have been made aware of the necessity to be involved in Kingdom work is what to do. What is it that God has specifically for you? How can you know you are walking the right path?

Not everyone has a "burning bush" experience where God rumbles a directive for your life. And not everyone is knocked off a horse and told to go get instruction from a particular minister or prophet. Most contact from God comes in much more subtle ways.

Many times it all begins with a burden: a gnawing at the soul that simply cannot be overcome. When Nehemiah finds out about the horrible condition of his homeland, and the disrepair to its walls and gates, he notes that "I sat down and wept, and mourned for many days..." (Nehemiah 1:4) His prayer for Jerusalem and Israel is one of repentance and petition for restoration.

As the believer takes note of the condition of our society, it can truly be said that "its wall... is... broken down, and its gates are burned with fire." (Nehemiah 1:3) In this calamity God reaches into the middle of this moment and says, "I want YOU. And I want you to..." He places a hurt or tugging inside your soul which you cannot deny. It may be the twinge you feel whenever you think of the condition of the Body of Christ and its complacency in reaching the lost or holding to its God-given standards.

It could be a pain experienced whenever you consider the millions of unborn that have been slaughtered by inconsiderate choices. It may rise up every time you hear of the undermining of the family structure that God has put in place. You may experience it every time you hear another ruling by the Supreme Court that undermines Christianity and true religious freedom. Or it may be a matter of "all of the above" and more.

This burden causes you to ask, "Why doesn't someone do something?!"

In the late nineties someone asked that very question within himself. The fallen nature of the nation had come to the attention of this man. He was a good citizen. He voted in every election for the person(s) that he knew would better represent his Christian values. He even delivered sermons every Sunday morning to his congregation to bring them to a closer relationship with

God. But something still ate at his soul which he could not get away from.

One day while in prayer, he cried out to God, "Why doesn't someone DO something?!" And in the deepest burden he had ever experienced he began to pray an intercessory prayer for those in government, the Church, and the citizens of this nation who had not only allowed this to happen, but were involved in actively bringing it to pass.

And in the midst of the "Why" prayer, God spoke to his heart. "I have chosen *you* to take a stand." And at that moment, I realized it was not up to *someone else* "out there" to become involved. It was up to *me*. I had to put myself into the battle. God was delivering His order to "fire!". It was *my* turn.

But how does someone even get involved in such a gigantic task? What can a pastor of a non-mega-church do to influence American society? What can *I* do?

You may be reading this and asking yourself that same general question. "What can *I* do? How do I begin? Yes, I feel this burden, and now I know what it is; but what should I do with it?"

The first action to take is to approach God in prayer. He knows what His plan for you is. Ask for direction in the next steps to take, and how to prepare for what is ahead. He will guide you.

Open yourself to what God places before you. When He plants a burden in your heart, He will also give you an awareness of opportunities if you will ask Him. Each local situation allows for a unique variety of settings for service.

In the late 1990's I was compelled to assist a local political party. I reviewed the platforms of the various parties, and was guided to the one which promoted my moral values best. At first my involvement was minimal: assisting with a phone bank for candidates I supported, and being a bit vocal among my peers. And by making myself available, God took it from there.

It was not long before a State Congressman asked if he could stop by and speak with me. A leader in my precinct had resigned due to a job-based move, and I had come to his attention somehow. I accepted the position of Precinct-Leader, and suddenly I was walking precincts and serving as part of the county party's "Central Committee". That congressman is now in the State Senate.

Once involved, I moved in the directions I felt led to pursue in order to effect change. Because of this God has opened doors that I, alone, could never have had presented before me. Leadership within the party and at the State House and Senate have asked to have the invocation delivered at their sessions. I have flown to Washington, D.C. to be involved in a "Watchmen on the Wall" conference, sponsored by the Family Research Council, and have participated in "Pastor's Day at the Capitol" in Colorado several times. At this point in time, I serve as the House District Chairman in my area, and continue to be open to God's continued direction.

The brief synopsis above only contains a small portion of what God has made available. And it all has been for His glory! A difference is being made, and it involves a pastor who could not even imagine the magnitude of events and services that would be presented to him.

This example is only offered for encouragement. You can rest assured that the only part personally played in this journey is being available for service, and taking steps when led to do so. Where the skills there at the beginning to carry out the tasks to be done? No. Is this a deserved path? No.

Reviewing the course which has been followed brings tears of thanksgiving to the God of heaven; for to Him is the power and the glory forever.

So where does your path begin? There are so many opportunities for service in whatever field of burden God has delivered into your care. Perhaps your spiritual mentor will have a few ideas. Perhaps God will give you a "burning bush"? If He did it for Moses, I assure you He can do it for you. Or perhaps it will come in a "still small voice" as it did for Elijah. (I Kings 19:11-13) Be open for Him to instruct you. And then be willing to step out of the boat.

One of my favorite scenes in any movie ever is in *Indiana Jones and the Last Crusade*[101]. In order to save his father's life, Indiana Jones must cross a massive chasm to retrieve the Holy Grail. The instructions tell him to take a "leap from the lion's head" out into the void ahead. He states to himself that this is a "leap of faith". Racing against time, he does not have time

---

[101] Lucas, George and Menno Meyjes, *Indiana Jones and the Last Crusade*. DVD. Screenplay by Jeffrey Boam, Directed by Steven Spielberg. Hollywood: Paramount Pictures, 1989.

to have a philosophical or theological discussion regarding what it really means to "step out". Muttering a prayer under his breath, he reaches out with a boot and steps down, surprised to find that there is a bridge that has been camouflaged to look like the surrounding walls which plummet an untold distance below.

Your "chasm" can be many things. It may be challenging friends on their viewpoints on matters which directly affect our society, or volunteering to serve in an agency which supports a biblical principle in which you feel burdened to be active.

You may find it in writing letters to government officials, or holding signs in front of abortion clinics. Or you could face a fearful chasm in approaching your spiritual leaders in challenging them to step up their involvement.

Maybe your leap of faith involves teaching a Sunday School class, or leading a Children's or Women's Ministry group. Maybe God has burdened you to perform in singing or other musical abilities to proclaim His Word. It could also come in the form of composing articles for newspapers and magazines, or in writing a book on the Christian foundations of America.

Whatever the giant is you may face, God is ready to have you take action. He is preparing the way. Once you have found your path, He awaits for you to step out.

You can find assurance in knowing that God has a plan for you. He will grant you whatever ability and power is necessary to complete the tasks He sets before you. "Being confident of this very thing, that He who has begun a good work in you will complete *it* until the day of Jesus Christ." (Philippians 1:6) You can do it! Others have gone before to prepare the way for your moment in time. IT'S YOUR TURN!!!

Addendum

Where to go to get involved

ACTION GROUPS*

FAMILY RESEARCH COUNCIL
801 G Street NW, Washington, D.C. 20001
(800) 225-4008
www.frc.org

FRC – WATCHMEN ON THE WALL
"Championing Pastors to Transform America"
Contact information as above
www.WatchmenPastors.org

The Black Robe Regiment
http://blackroberegiment.ning.com

Alliance Defending Freedom
15100 N. 90th Street
Scottsdale, AZ 85260
(800) 225-4008
www.alliancedefendingfreedom.org

CitizenLink
8655 Explorer Drive|
Colorado Springs, CO 80920
(866) 655.4545
www.citizenlink.com

National Right to Life
http://nrlc.org/

* The action groups listed have not endorsed
this book, actual or implied.

FEDERAL GOVERNMENT CONNECTIONS

White House switchboard

Comments: 202-456-1111
Switchboard: 202-456-1414
Visitor's Office: 202-456-2121

Write a letter to the President

The White House
1600 Pennsylvania Avenue NW
Washington, DC 20500

SENATE

For correspondence to U.S. Senators:
Office of Senator (Name)
United States Senate
Washington, D.C. 20510
For correspondence to Senate Committees:
(Name of Committee)
United States Senate
Washington, D.C. 20510

By Telephone
Alternatively, you may phone the United States
Capitol switchboard at (202) 224-3121.
A switchboard operator will connect you directly
with the Senate office you request.
Website
www.senate.gov

HOUSE OF REPRESENTATIVES

U.S. House of Representatives
Washington, DC 20515
(202) 224-3121
Website
www.house.gov

STATE HOUSE CONNECTIONS
**<most state houses allow you to connect with
the governor through a form at their website>**

ALABAMA
Governor
http://governor.alabama.gov

Legislature
www.legislature.state.al.us

ALASKA
Governor
www.gov.state.ak.us

Legislature
http://w3.legis.state.ak.us

ARIZONA
Governor
http://azgovernor.gov/contact.asp

Legislature
www.azleg.gov

ARKANSAS
Governor
http://governor.arkansas.gov

Legislature
www.arkleg.state.ar.us

CALIFORNIA
Governor
http://gov.ca.gov/home.php

Legislature
www.legislature.ca.gov

COLORADO
Governor
www.colorado.gov/governor

Legislature
www.leg.state.co.us

CONNECTICUT
Governor
www.governor.ct.gov

Legislature
www.cga.ct.gov

DELAWARE
Governor
http://governor.delaware.gov

Legislature
http://legis.delaware.gov

FLORIDA
Governor
www.flgov.com/contact-governor

Legislature
www.leg.state.fl.us

GEORGIA
Governor
http://gov.georgia.gov

Legislature
www.legis.ga.gov

HAWAII
Governor
http://azgovernor.gov/contact.asp

Legislature
www.capitol.hawaii.gov

IDAHO
Governor
http://gov.idaho.gov

Legislature
http://legislature.idaho.gov

ILLINOIS
Governor
www2.illinois.gov/gov

Legislature
www.ilga.gov

INDIANA
Governor
www.in.gov/gov

Legislature
www.in.gov/legislative

IOWA
Governor
https://governor.iowa.gov/contact

Legislature
www.legis.iowa.gov/Contacts/legisContact.aspx

KANSAS
Governor
www.kansas.gov

Legislature
www.kslegislature.org

KENTUCKY
Governor
http://governor.ky.gov

Legislature
www.lrc.ky.gov

LOUISIANA
Governor
www.gov.la.gov

Legislature
www.legis.la.gov

MAINE
Governor
www.maine.gov/governor

Legislature
www.maine.gov/legis

MARYLAND
Governor
www.governor.maryland.gov

Legislature
http://mgaleg.maryland.gov

MASSACHUSETTES

Governor

www.mass.gov/governor

Legislature

https://malegislature.gov

MICHIGAN

Governor

www.michigan.gov

Legislature

www.legislature.mi.gov

MINNESOTA

Governor

https://mn.gov/governor/contact-us

Legislature

www.leg.state.mn.us/leg/legdir.aspx

MISSISSIPPI

Governor

www.ms.gov

Legislature

www.legislature.ms.gov

MISSOURI
Governor
http://governor.mo.gov/contact

Legislature
www.moga.mo.gov

MONTANA
Governor
http://governor.mt.gov

Legislature
http://leg.mt.gov

NEBRASKA
Governor
www.governor.nebraska.gov

Legislature
http://nebraskalegislature.gov

NEVADA
Governor
http://gov.nv.gov

Legislature
www.leg.state.nv.us

NEW HAMPSHIRE

Governor

http://governor.nh.gov

Legislature

www.nh.gov

NEW JERSEY

Governor

www.state.nj.us/governor

Legislature

www.njleg.state.nj.us

NEW MEXICO

Governor

www.governor.state.nm.us

Legislature

www.nmlegis.gov/lcs

NEW YORK

Governor

www.governor.ny.gov

Legislature

http://assembly.state.ny.us

NORTH CAROLINA
Governor
www.governor.state.nc.us

Legislature
www.ncga.state.nc.us

NORTH DAKOTA
Governor
http://governor.nd.gov

Legislature
www.legis.nd.gov

OHIO
Governor
www.governor.ohio.gov

Legislature
www.legislature.state.oh.us

OKLAHOMA
Governor
www.ok.gov/governor

Legislature
www.oklegislature.gov

OREGON
Governor
www.oregon.gov/gov

Legislature
www.leg.state.or.us

PENNSYLVANIA
Governor
http://www.governor.state.pa.us

Legislature
www.legis.state.pa.us

RHODE ISLAND
Governor
www.governor.ri.gov

Legislature
www.rilin.state.ri.us

SOUTH CAROLINA
Governor
http://governor.sc.gov

Legislature
www.scstatehouse.gov

SOUTH DAKOTA
Governor
http://sd.gov/governor

Legislature
http://legis.state.sd.us

TENNESSEE
Governor
www.tn.gov/governor

Legislature
www.capitol.tn.gov

TEXAS
Governor
http://governor.state.tx.us

Legislature
www.capitol.state.tx.us

UTAH
Governor
http://utah.gov/governor

Legislature
www.utah.gov/government/legislative.html

VERMONT
Governor
http://governor.vermont.gov

Legislature
www.leg.state.vt.us

VIRGINIA
Governor
www.governor.virginia.gov

Legislature
http://virginiageneralassembly.gov

WASHINGTON
Governor
www.governor.wa.gov

Legislature
www.leg.wa.gov

WEST VIRGINIA
Governor
www.governor.wv.gov

Legislature
www.legis.state.wv.us

WISCONSIN
Governor
www.wisgov.state.wi.us

Legislature
http://legis.wisconsin.gov

WYOMING
Governor
http://governor.wy.gov

Legislature
http://legisweb.state.wy.us